# NAPI

# NAPI
## *The Trickster*

## HUGH A. DEMPSEY
### ILLUSTRATED BY ALYSSA KOSKI

Victoria | Vancouver | Calgary

Heritage House Publishing Company Ltd.
heritagehouse.ca

CATALOGUING INFORMATION AVAILABLE
FROM LIBRARY AND ARCHIVES CANADA
978-1-77203-217-8 (pbk)
978-1-77203-218-5 (epub)

Edited by Lenore Hietkamp
Proofread by Lesley Cameron
Cover design by Jacqui Thomas
Interior design by Colin Parks
Cover and interior illustrations by Alyssa Koski

The interior of this book was produced on 100% post-consumer recycled
paper, processed chlorine free, and printed with vegetable-based inks.

We acknowledge the financial support of the Government of Canada
through the Canada Book Fund (CBF) and the Canada Council for
the Arts, and the Province of British Columbia through the British
Columbia Arts Council and the Book Publishing Tax Credit.

22 21 20 19 18    1 2 3 4 5

Printed in Canada

# CONTENTS

PUBLISHER'S NOTE

This collection of stories about Napi the trickster contains graphic violence, including scenes of rape and murder. The author explains that when these stories were recorded at the turn of the twentieth century, the Blackfoot people told them to audiences of all ages, but today the stories are more suitable for adults than children.

# FOREWORD

I was introduced to Hugh Dempsey by my father, James Gladstone, at an Indian Association of Alberta meeting on February 5, 1950. My father was the president of the IAA at that time and Hugh was the provincial editor of the *Edmonton Bulletin*. For the Native peoples of Canada, the IAA was seeking such rights as family allowance, old age security, and hunting.

Hugh, at twenty-one, was reported to be the youngest editor on a daily newspaper in Canada. That is when he began a lifetime of devotion and dedication to the Indian people. Thinking back, it was the beginning of both his and my father's careers, which blossomed throughout their lives, demonstrating a dedication that persists for Hugh to this day.

Sometimes I pinch myself when I think of the wonderful people who were in the twilight of their years in the 1950s. There were men and women such at Bobtail Chief, Suzette Eagle Ribs, Sinew Feet, John Cotton, Jack Low Horn, Jim White Bull, Vickie McHugh, Jack Black Horse, One Gun, Chief Shot Both Sides, and the list goes on and on. While Dad listened to them speaking of their rights, Hugh spoke to them about their experiences and their stories of bygone days. Some had actually been at the last battles held around Fort Whoop-Up.

At a young age, I noticed Hugh's mind was like a sponge. Not only were people willing to share their knowledge with him, but they were fascinated that someone was interested in hearing their stories and reminiscing with them.

Hugh wrote about the knowledge that was passed on to him. First were the stories relating to the history of the Blackfoot tribes, and then the stories about culture and religion. I have been told that the information he gathered back then was of such value that the young people of today are using it, as will future generations. He hopes his work will inspire young Native people not only to learn of the colourful backgrounds of their ancestors but also to become writers themselves.

Hugh records a history that otherwise would have died with the Blood, Peigan, and Blackfoot elders. I am so grateful that I was there when all this was unfolding. And for being asked to voice my humble opinion.

**Pauline Gladstone Dempsey**, Calgary, Alberta
Daughter of Senator James Gladstone
Member of the Blood Tribe, Blackfoot First Nation
Recipient of the Chief David Crowchild Memorial Award (1987)
    and Alberta Achievement Award (1988)

# INTRODUCTION

When I first went among the Blackfoot sixty-four years ago, I was impressed by the richness of their history and culture. And when I married into the Blood tribe, lifelong friendships were established with people like Gerald Tailfeathers and Everett Soop. Then, through my father-in-law, James Gladstone, I met the elders who were the repositories of tribal lore, and I found them more than happy to share their knowledge with me. At first I concentrated on the history of the three tribes—the Bloods, the Blackfoot, and the Peigans—and the elders provided graphic images of what life was like in the buffalo days. My research carried me forward to contemporary issues and then backward to mythical figures such as Napi, the Old Man of the Blackfoot.

Napi is a creature of legend, a figure that appears prominently in mythology, sometimes as a quasi-creator, sometimes a fool, and sometimes a brutal murderer. He was generally considered to appear in the image of man. He personified strength through his supernatural powers, but his power was not reined in by reason.[1] He was a trickster, deceiving everyone he came into contact with, frustrating them, confusing them, and even killing them. I learned that Napi was credited with creating the earth and everything on it, but he was not a hero figure. Rather, he possessed all the weaknesses and strengths of man but in a supernatural way.

Over the years I have heard many Napi stories, sometimes in the style of the old people, and at other times heavily laced with aspects of Christianity. In some of the modernized stories, there was even confusion between Napi and Santa Claus. The stories told here are ones that were told at the turn of the twentieth century, when they were less affected by influences of the modern world. No stories were omitted because of modern sensitivities. Rather, virtually the whole body of Napi stories is included: tales of wisdom, foolishness, sex, greed, pity, murder, and generosity. They are rife with adventure, serving as object lessons for the young or as amusement during dark evenings in camp.

## NAPI IN BLACKFOOT CULTURE

Although Napi is said to have created many of the objects and creatures on earth, and even earth itself, he was never considered to be god-like. If anyone asked a Blackfoot if they ever prayed to Napi, the question would be greeted with hilarity. Napi was superhuman and could do miraculous things, but he was never revered. How could they feel devotion for someone who killed babies, disfigured animals, and roasted prairie dogs alive? How could they respect someone who was unbelievably foolish and naive? Anthropologists have called him a trickster/creator, which is probably as good an expression as any. He was man personified, for in almost any Napi story one can see a real counterpart in human form.[2]

The Napi stories, according to the ethnologist Clark Wissler and his local interpreter and assistant David Duvall, "recite the absurd, humorous, obscene, and brutal incidents in the Old Man's career."[3] The authors say that the stories are not the basis for any ritualistic or ceremonial use, as with the star myths, but they do contain a significant amount of detail on Blackfoot material culture from an early period. There are references to stone knives, mauls, digging sticks, scalps, baby swings, and buffalo jumps as well as accounts of making weapons, dressing skins, and cooking.

People who hear Napi stories are seldom sympathetic to the situations he has created for himself, nor do they always understand his motives. Rather, the more outrageous and foolhardy Napi's actions, the more a Blackfoot audience would laugh. No matter how desperate his situation, they knew he would escape.

Napi was not just a simple buffoon. His adventures sometimes included a lesson for the listener. Harvest the bullberries by thrashing the bush; don't unnecessarily kill the female of the species; honour the women in the camp; do not seek unwanted or illicit sex or your actions will either backfire on you or create anger among those around you.

One can learn from the stories how Napi made the earth and everything on it yet got into trouble when he started tinkering with his own creation. In Napi's world, he used a combination of strategy and supernatural power to win at gambling or to escape from a perilous situation. And when he fled he did not hesitate to ridicule his pursuers. Another lesson learned from Napi was to be careful whom you trust. The ducks trusted Napi and he wrung their necks; the prairie dogs trusted him and he roasted them. When any creature was asked to close its eyes, it was usually the last thing it did. Similarly, no one could expect kindness if they did Napi a favour. The nighthawks learned this after they saved him from a rolling rock and he disfigured their babies, while the birch tree's bark was slashed after it saved him from being blown away. In both instances he accused them of spoiling his fun.

Napi had not created a perfect world, and he became an imperfect figure within it. But those in the stories and those who hear the stories realize this. If he were perfect he would be boring, and Napi was anything but boring. Gathering around a campfire in the darkness of the evening, people heard how Napi blundered and schemed as he wandered through Blackfoot country. They laughed when they heard how he had been outwitted by a lame wolf and how a creek was named to commemorate the event. They learned how Napi tried to fly with the geese, but he looked down when he was told not to and fell to the earth. A creature whose excessive actions knew no bounds, he was the perfect subject for telling, listening, and enjoying.

A common phrase in Napi stories is the comment from an animal that "it is not hard to do." Whenever listeners heard that statement, they knew that Napi was in deep trouble. For Napi, nothing was easy. While the stories are sometimes even savage, McClintock observed that everyone "always liked the Old Man stories, because of their power to entertain and make people laugh."[4]

Some Napi stories explain how certain creatures and plants were affected by his experiences. For example, bobcats are shaped the way they are because of Napi's anger, and momentous decisions about life or death come from actions. The continuation of the species is an ongoing feature of the Napi stories. In the account where the elk are being lured to their death over a cliff, George Bird Grinnell, who recorded stories of the Indigenous peoples in the area, notes that one cow was left:

> "They have all jumped but you," said Old Man. "Come on, you will like it."
>
> "Take pity on me," said the cow. "I am very heavy, and I am afraid to jump."
>
> "Go away, then," said Old Man; "go and live. Then some day there will be plenty of elk again."[5]

One implication of this story is that the small groups of animals Napi met in his travels were the only ones in existence, and that the killing of a female could wipe out an entire species. It was also a warning to the Blackfoot hunter about unnecessarily killing cows when bulls were available.

In the late twentieth century, some Blackfoot considered Napi to be simply an evil person whose antics were the source of ribald entertainment. In everyday conversation, Napi's name became synonymous with immorality. In the 1950s, for example, there was a Napi Bar on the Blackfeet reservation in Montana. In 1960, when the author was shown a boulder effigy monument of Napi's resting place, bawdy comments centred around the length of his penis. Over the years, moral sensitivities have caused some storytellers to "clean up" Napi tales, so that the nighthawks struck the rolling stone with their beaks, rather than farting on it, and Napi gave a chickadee a heavy necklace to hold, rather than his penis. Other people have tried to find a relationship between Napi and Christianity, seeing Napi as the devil.

Some believe that Napi stories should be told only at night. However, rather than being a restriction, this is probably because the daylight hours were occupied with hunting, food preparation, and other matters that kept men and women busy. Only after the sun had gone down, with a small fire lighting the tipi, was there leisure time for telling stories. According to Wissler and Duvall, no one was restricted to telling stories only "at certain times of the year," and no stories were peculiar to being told by women or men, "any one being at liberty to render any myth whatsoever."[6]

The longtime existence of Napi stories is confirmed by the place names in Alberta that relate to his adventures. One important landmark commemorating Napi is the Old Man River (Napia-otsi-kagh-tsipi, Where the Old Man Gambled),[7] named for an event on its upper waters where Napi gambled for control of the land. Tongue Creek or Tongue Flag Creek (Matsin-awastam),[8] in the Nanton area, is named after the account of Napi being tricked and having all his food stolen. Included were elk tongues that had been placed on poles like flags to keep them away from mice. And the town of Okotoks (meaning "rock") is named for the big rock that chased Napi and was split in two by the nighthawks. The rock itself is a short distance southwest of the town.

At a site on the Red Deer River near its confluence with Rosebud Creek is a stone boulder effigy monument known as Where Napi Slept (Napia-okanes).[9] The monument consists of stones laid out on the ground in the shape of a man, with arms and legs outstretched and with a penis that is almost twice as long as the legs. This is in keeping with Napi myths about his power to extend the length of his penis. A second site with the same name exists on the Bow River, just south of Crowfoot Siding. It is smaller but of similar construction and with the extended penis. The rainbow (*kinakaka'atsis*, "small ropes") is a synonym for Napi's penis. According to Wissler and Duvall, "Old Man's genitals are also spoken of as a lariat. The rainbow is often designated as such, using either term apparently at random. However, the usual idea is, that his genitals are used as a lariat to rope the clouds."[10] Mike Mountain Horse, a member of the Blood people, added, "The appearance of a rainbow during a shower was an indication that the storm would subside in a short time, for, in the words of the Indian belief, 'Napi has lassoed the storm.'"[11]

West of Nanton in the foothills is Men's Buffalo Jump, or Nina-piskun, where men hunted buffalo and lived alone before discovering marriage. Napi found them at this site and led them north to Women's Buffalo Jump, or Akipiskun (on Squaw Coulee, three kilometres northwest of Cayley), where the women hunted without the assistance of men. In 1952, heavy rainfall flowed in torrents down the side of the coulee, exposing layers of bones and ash. The Women's Buffalo Jump site was brought to the attention of archaeologists from the Glenbow Foundation who undertook excavations in 1958 and 1959. Going down more than fifteen feet through layers of ash and bones, they determined that the site was at least two thousand years old.[12]

In an attempt to find information about the antiquity of the site, people from the Glenbow spoke to John Cotton, an eighty-two-year-old member of the Blood people, who said,

> In the early days of the world, the men and the women used to travel in separate camps. The men had their chief and the women had theirs. One day Napi called the men together and said: "Why should we live apart from the women? If we all live together, then we can spend our time hunting and going to war, while the women can do the cooking and tanning of hides." The men thought it was a good idea, so Napi went in search of the women. He found them near the foothills, where they all lived in a large camp. Nearby they had a buffalo jump, which was their main source of food. This was the Women's Buffalo Jump near Cayley.[13]

The earliest known reference to Women's Buffalo Jump is in a winter-count for 1842-43, when a Blood chief named Bad Head recorded, "When at Women's Buffalo Jump / Many in one camp" ("Itake-piskiiopi akokinu").[14]

Another site referring to Napi, called Napi's Slide, is located at the edge of the Rocky Mountains north of the Bow River. According to R.N. Wilson, Napi and Kit Fox were travelling about the country when they came to the top of a high hill. "Napi slid to the bottom instead of walking down," he writes, "and, it being a stony place, he brought down a great bank of stones to the bottom with him."[15] Horatio Hale adds, "Any one can see at the present day the place where Napiw came down by sliding."[16]

Names for at least two creatures are based on Napi stories. The bobcat, or lynx, is known as Nap-iyo, or Old Man Greasy Stepping. This is based on the account of a bobcat stealing Napi's roasted prairie dogs and being easily followed because of his greasy footsteps. Once apprehended, Napi punished the animal by flattening his face, stretching his hind legs, and applying pubic hairs to his face as whiskers. Similarly, the nighthawk (*Chordeiles minor*) is known as Pisto ("fart"), based upon the story in which a rock pursued Napi and his life was saved by nighthawks that swooped down and farted on the rock, each time breaking off a part of it. They finally succeeded in splitting the rock in half and stopping it.

If nothing else, these animal and place names reflect the antiquity and originality of the Napi stories. They also indicate that many incidents took place in southern Alberta in a fairly confined region adjacent to the foothills. This might be an indication of the long residency of the Blackfoot tribes in this region, supported by other Napi stories telling of the creation of the Sweetgrass Hills and Chief Mountain.

Usually, there are no accounts of life before the flood, but there are exceptions. The Peigan chief Bull Plume said, "Look, don't you see on all the high hills many stones placed in a circle, places of old camps? This is where the Indians went to camp on these high places to try to save themselves from the flood."[17] Stories that attempt to connect Napi with the world before the flood are usually adaptations of other Blackfoot legends.

As for his creation, one informant said, "No one made Old Man; he always existed."[18] John Maclean, a missionary, stated that no one knew "the manner of his birth, nor the place from whence he came."[19] One origin version says Napi was created from the mist. There he experimented with his own form until he was satisfied with it. For example, he first placed his penis and testicles on top of his head, but found this unwieldy.

The usual stories of Napi begin with him floating on a raft, often with three animals: a beaver, a muskrat, and an otter.[20] As the entire surface of the earth was covered with water, Napi sent each creature in turn to dive to the bottom to bring up some mud. The beaver and otter failed, but at last the muskrat was successful and came to the surface with a small amount of earth in its claw. Napi took this and rolled it into a ball that grew and grew until it fell off the raft and into the water, where it continued to grow. The animals that were with him ran onto the new land and became its first inhabitants.

According to Grinnell, the raft was grounded in the present state of Wyoming, and from there Napi made his way north.[21] As he went, he created prairies, mountains, trees, and rivers, populating the area with all kinds of animals and birds. He gambled with a supernatural being from across the mountains and lost an east–west mountain range. He kept the Sweetgrass Hills but moved the rest to form a range of the Rocky Mountains. He also gambled for control of the buffalo. This time he won, and the buffalo were kept on the east side of the mountains. During these adventures Napi was in his serious period, a time when he created and played no tricks.

Once this phase had passed, Napi began travelling through his newly created land, meeting with animals and revealing another side of his personality, "a combination of strength, weakness, wisdom, folly, child-ishness, and malice."[22] Story after story recounts how he played tricks on animals, how they sometimes outsmarted him, and how he could be vicious and cruel.

After a while Napi became bored and wanted companionship, so he created a woman and a child. After he had given them life, Napi discussed their future with the woman. He suggested that when a person died they would rise again after four days. The woman disagreed, saying that when they died, they died forever. Later, when the child died, the woman wanted to change the rules, but Napi would not agree. In the beginning, Napi also had suggestions to make life easier—that when a child was born, they could run around after four days, that people would eat the sap from trees that would always be there, that animals would come to life after four days, that there would be wild berries all year round, that the skins from animals would not need to be tanned, and when wood burned it would not need to be replaced. In each instance the woman disagreed. "And," concluded Jean-Louis Levern, who recorded this story, "it is thus by the strong will of the woman, [that] all is in the worst possible state in the world."[23]

The woman ultimately left Napi and began to create women in her own likeness. Meanwhile, Napi started to make men and turned them loose on the prairies. Later, when he visited them, he discovered they were being attacked and eaten by buffalo. He then taught them to make weapons and to kill the buffalo. He also showed them how to light fires to cook their food and to use the hides to make shelters. Meanwhile, the woman had taught her creations the same lessons, but she observed how they took pride in quillworking and caring for their lodges.

One day, Napi happened upon the women who were killing buffalo at a buffalo jump. He learned how they hated to hunt but loved to be busy in their lodges. Napi was aware that the men were just the opposite: they liked to hunt but took terrible care of their shelters. This gave him the brilliant idea of bringing the men and women together. This was arranged, but Napi failed to get a woman for himself and in the end he was turned into a pine tree.

For many, the story ends there, but others say his adventures continued, including incidents with a wife and mother-in-law. Finally, he left the Blackfoot people. Some say he went across the mountains but other storytellers believe he went east, where he was captured by white people and forever became their prisoner. According to Grinnell,

> Old Man can never die. Long ago he left the Blackfeet and went away to the West, disappearing in the mountains. Before his departure he told them that he would always take care of them, and some day would return. Even now [in 1892], many of the old people believe that he spoke the truth, and that some day he will come back, and will bring with him the buffalo, which they believe the white men have hidden. It is sometimes said, however, that when he left them he told them also that, when he returned, he would find them changed—a different people and living in a different way from that which they practised when he went away. Others have said that when Napi disappeared he went to the East.[24]

There are some who believe that the events that occurred after the pine tree incident are later additions to the original Napi story. They feel that the story really ends when men and women came together, after which time they could produce their own progeny and establish their own rules of society. After this, Napi was no longer needed.

## STAR MYTHS

A considerable amount of Blackfoot religion is based upon star myths involving people who interacted with star people or became stars themselves. Events that marked their lives often became the basis for ritualistic or religious practices. For example, there is a story about Crow Arrow turning into a crow and herding the buffalo away from the people; this action is copied by the sacred Motokix, Old Women's Society, with a pecking ritual at the end of their dance. Wissler and Duvall point out that Napi was never associated with such ritualism, so whenever he appears in a star myth, he is someone's later addition and does not belong in the story.

In one tale recorded by Wissler and Duvall, "During the flood, Old Man was sitting on the highest mountain with all the beasts. The flood was caused by the above people, because the baby (a fungus) of the woman who married a star was heedlessly torn to pieces by an Indian child."[25] This story is adapted from a star myth that tells of a young woman who married the Morning Star, the son of the Sun and the Moon. She lived happily with him in the sky and had a baby boy. One day she dug up a large turnip and through the hole it left in the clouds, she could see her camp below. Suddenly homesick, she returned to Morning Star's lodge, and he knew at once what had happened. He told her she would have to return to her people and that the Sun would teach her the ceremonies of the Sun Dance.

Before the woman was lowered down to earth, the Sun changed the baby into a puffball and told her that after the first Sun Dance the baby would resume its form. However, while she was teaching the ceremonies to the Blackfoot, a young boy found the puffball in her robes and squeezed the life out of it. The woman sadly continued her teaching, and the first

Sun Dance was held. That is the original story, but later storytellers have tried to insert Napi into the account—a place where he does not belong.

There are other questionable accounts where Napi and star myths collide. For example, Napi was said in one story to be the brother of Morning Star, and their parents were the Sun and the Moon. The Sun became suspicious of his wife and followed her into the woods one day where he saw her tap on an old tree. A snake in the form of a handsome man came out and they made love. Next day, the Sun told his wife he was going hunting but instead went to the tree and killed the snake. When the Moon learned of it, she took her stone axe and pursued her husband. He fled to the sky and asked Morning Star to accompany him and protect him while Napi was sent out to create the land and everything on it. When Napi arrived on earth everything was black, but then the Sun appeared and caused the land to flourish. Meanwhile the Moon was still pursuing her husband and when she appeared, the Sun fled. This created night and day. The Moon said, "If I ever overtake you, the world will come to an end."[26] However, in the original account, Morning Star had no brother and Napi's name does not appear. These were quasi-Christian additions.

The telling of a classic myth relating to the Twin Stars has also had Napi inserted into it, in two different roles. In the original version, a man's wife was pregnant with twins. He had to go hunting and warned his wife not to invite anyone in, for he had had a bad dream about an evil man. The woman did not listen, and when the stranger appeared, she invited him in and fed him. The man did not want to eat from a bowl or from the floor, but consented to eat from the top of the woman's belly. Then, while cutting the meat, he slashed open the woman's stomach, killing her, and the twins jumped out. The stranger put one near the ashes of the fireplace and called him Ashes Chief, and the other he hid behind the curtain and called Stuck Behind.

When the father returned he found his wife dead and the babies crying. He pursued the mysterious stranger, and when he caught him, the man said he would give him the power to bring the woman back to life. He presented the husband with the Four-Tail Lodge design and the songs and rituals that went with it. He then gave Ashes Chief to a rock to raise and Stuck Behind he gave to some beavers. At this point, the stranger disappears from the story, but considering his bizarre actions and supernatural powers, some felt he must have been Napi. But, in fact, he was not. This is a story about ritualism and the eventual transformation of the twins into stars.

Further on in the story, the boys were fifteen years old when Napi again was added to the account. In the original story, one twin became good and the other evil. The good twin located buffalo that had been trapped in a cave by Crow Arrow and, with the help of a Blackfoot, set them free. Then the good twin joined his brother in the sky and they became the Twin Stars. Some storytellers have included Napi in the story at the point where the people were starving.[27] In their account, it was Napi, not the good twin, who was joined by the Blackfoot and found the buffalo. Napi turned himself into a puppy and his companion into a digging stick. The two were found by Crow Arrow's daughter, who took them home.[28] Next day, the woman and girl went out to dig for wild turnips. When they approached the entrance to Crow Arrow's cave, Napi realized that this was where the buffalo were imprisoned. Quickly he and the Blackfoot went inside and drove the animals out.

Crow Arrow turned himself into a white crow to drive the buffalo back, but Napi turned himself into a beaver and lay down as if dead.[29] The crow came along and started pecking him, at which time Napi captured him and tied him to the smoke hole until he turned black. Then, rubbing the bird's beak in the dirt, he said, "This is what you will eat in the future and as you have so much to say you will be dumb in future as far as talking Blackfoot is concerned."[30] This segment of the myth included Napi, yet it is incorrect and not a good fit. The exploits of Napi are seldom surrounded by such heroics and sense of purpose. Napi stories were not the source of ritualism such as found in this account.

## EARLY REFERENCES

The earliest known written reference to Napi dates from 1792, when the trader Peter Fidler travelled through the upper waters of the Oldman River in southern Alberta. On December 31 he noted,

Then continued our way close along the bank of the river which is very rocky but a narrow pass betwixt the water & the high perpendicular rocks of the Mountain, S ⅓ of a Mile. A place here called Naw peu och eta cots [Napi/ Where He Gambled] from whence this river Derives its name . . . It is a place where Indians formerly assembled here to play at a particular Game with by rolling a small hoop of 4 Inches diameter & darting an Arrow out of the hand after it & those that put he arrow within the hoop while rolling along is reckoned to have gamed . . .

On my enquiring concerning the origin of this spot, the Indians . . . said that a White man (what they universally call Europeans) came from the South many ages ago, & built this for the Indians to Play at, that is different nations whom he wished to meet here annually & bury all animosities betwixt the different Tribes, by assembling & playing together. They also say that this same person made the Buffalo, on purpose for the Indians. They describe him as a very old white headed man & several more things very ridiculous.[31]

Fidler also provided a sketch of the site, showing an oval configuration of stones about thirty yards long and ten yards wide, with nine stone piles outside the circle and one stone pile and three circular placements within the oval. It seems possible that to play the hoop and arrow game, the person throwing the hoop would be at the north or narrow end of the oval and that the players would have some twenty yards within which they could throw their arrows. The arrows would be thrown just as the hoop was falling. McClintock describes the game:

The wheel was rolled over a smooth and level course, each player throwing an arrow at it. The points were counted according to the position of the arrows when the wheel stopped. Its origin is very ancient and it is often mentioned in old stories and legends.[32]

In 1811, the fur trader Alexander Henry mentions a story about Napi:

> The ideas the Blackfeet have of the creation and a future
> state are much confused. The following information, which
> I obtained from old Painted Feather, was all I could collect:
> At first the world was one body of water inhabited by only
> one great white man and his wife, who had no children.
> This man, in the course of time, made the earth, divided the
> waters into lakes and rivers, and formed the range of the
> Rocky mountains; after which he made the beasts, birds,
> fishes, and every other living creature.[33]

Like Fidler, Henry translated the word "Napi" as white man. The
Blackfoot at the time of first contact saw a relationship between Napi
and Europeans, observing how the white man could easily make fire,
shoot missiles through the air, and possess miraculous objects made
of iron. Viewing these newcomers and their mysterious ways, they
immediately compared them with their own trickster, whom they called
Napikwan. The name is still used to refer to a white man, and Napiaki
to a white woman. This is perhaps why Fidler and Henry also referred
to Napi as a white man.

In 1854, James Doty, with the Stevens United States railway exploring
expedition, also commented on Napi:

> The Blackfeet have only one Tradition concerning their
> origin. They say that the first inhabitants of their country
> were an old man and his wife, that this Old Man wandered
> through the country for many years, creating Mountains,
> Lakes, Rivers, Plains, etc., and stocking them with game.
> They say it was his amusement to play at marbles with enor-
> mous boulders or nodules of sand stone and they point out
> several places said to be his play-ground. Finally he created
> the Blackfeet Nation, as numerous as they at present exist,
> and then departed they know not where. This tradition is
> said to have been handed down from their ancestors and

is the only ideas they have of whence they came or how
they were created.[34]

By the 1870s and 1880s, missionaries and scientists began to show an
interest in Blackfoot mythology, including Napi stories. In 1874 Albert
Lacombe, a Catholic priest, provided a confusing account that indicated
the Sun spirit and Napi were one and the same. He claimed that Napi
eventually left the earth and went to the sun. No reference was made
to his erratic behaviour; in fact, he is described as "Napé, le Parfait."[35]
By 1885, however, Lacombe had become more acquainted with the real
Napi, saying he "comes down from the high position of creator to a
much lower one, and appears not unlike to a buffoon and treacherous
rascal."[36] Lacombe relates the story of the flood and creation of men
and women but he continues to associate Napi with the Sun spirit. He
adds, "The whole of this is confused enough in the minds of the Indians
to render them unable to give, when questioned, exact explanations."[37]
The confusion was, of course, with the missionary, not the Blackfoot.

A fellow priest, Émile Petitot, published *Traditions indiennes du
Canada nord-ouest* in 1886, in which two pages are devoted to Napi.
Petitot's information came from a Cree Metis at Fort Pitt in 1873.[38]

In the mid-1880s, the British Association for the Advancement
of Science became interested in the Indigenous people of northwest
Canada, and enlisted Horatio Hale and Edward F. Wilson, a missionary,
to investigate the Blackfoot and then present their findings. Hale's report
of 1885 was based largely upon information provided by Lacombe and
John Maclean, another missionary. Using their information, he was more
intent upon finding a non-Blackfoot source for most of their beliefs and
ceremonies than in speaking of their culture. Wilson, for his 1887 report,
interviewed Crowfoot, head chief of the Blackfoot, and other leaders
from that tribe. Crowfoot scoffed at the Association's popular belief that
the Blackfoot had come from the Manitoba region and asserted that
they had lived for generations in the land they now occupied.

Another leader, Big Plume, told Wilson that Napi had made the
sun and created night and day. "Napi is very old every winter," he said,
"but he becomes young every spring. He has travelled all along the

Rocky Mountains, and there are various marks on the mountains which remain as relics of his presence."[39] He said Napi made the first woman from his lower rib on the right side—an obvious reference to Christian belief—and later created men and brought them together in marriage.

John Maclean, a Methodist missionary to the Blood people from 1880 to 1889 who published a number of papers in scientific journals in the 1880s and 1890s, mentions Napi in his paper "Blackfoot Mythology," which appeared in the *Journal of American Folk-Lore* in 1893.[40] Maclean believed that "the separation of the tribes, the rapid settlement of the country by the white people, the death of many of the old chiefs, and the depressed spirits of the people have seriously impaired the purity of the folk-lore of the natives."[41] He made a point of gathering his information from the elders, as "the younger members of the tribe could not be relied upon to relate these myths accurately."[42]

The 1890s marked the beginning of the serious collecting of Napi stories, both for scientific study and for popular consumption. The first comprehensive collection of stories, *Blackfoot Lodge Tales*, was published in 1892 by George Bird Grinnell.[43] Ten years earlier Grinnell had met James Willard Schultz, later a noted author of young people's fiction, and through him he met members of the South Peigans in Montana. With the help of Schultz he collected information on the history and culture of the Blackfoot people. *Blackfoot Lodge Tales* became a classic and has gone through several reprints. The stories have stood the test of time and its contents on all aspects of Blackfoot life are as relevant today as they were when they were published. Grinnell then followed with a second book, *Blackfeet Indian Stories*, published in 1913[44]; most legends in this publication were rewrites from his earlier book.

In the early 1890s, Robert N. Wilson, a former member of the North-West Mounted Police and an Indian trader, began collecting stories from his store adjacent to the Blood Reserve. Inspired by the work of his neighbour, John Maclean, he assembled a comprehensive collection of Napi stories but never had them published. The value of Wilson's accounts lies in their extensiveness, the relatively early date of their collection, and Wilson's fluency in the Blackfoot language.

Another unpublished set of Napi stories was collected by Jean-Louis Levern, a Catholic priest, between 1907 and 1925.[45] Levern served on all three Blackfoot reserves in southern Alberta and was fluent in the language. Most of his stories, handwritten in French, appear to have been collected from the North Peigans. They are now in the Oblate collection at the Provincial Archives of Alberta in Edmonton. Levern includes about a dozen Napi stories as well as star myths and stories dealing with ritualist origins. Interspersed are Catholic articles, such as "Why Do the Blackfoot Wish to Have Priests Among Them?" and "A Beautiful Death [after conversion]." The Napi stories themselves appear to be free of any Christian bias.

Just after the turn of the century, four studies by professionals were published. These were *Mythology of the Blackfoot Indians* by the ethnologist Clark Wissler and his assistant David C. Duvall, published in 1908; *Original Blackfoot Texts,* by Christianus C. Uhlenbeck, a linguist, published in 1911; *A New Series of Blackfoot Texts,* also by Uhlenbeck, published in 1912; and *Blackfoot Texts,* by Jan de Josselin de Jong, Uhlenbeck's student, published in 1914.[46]

Wissler was noted for his work among the northern Plains tribes, particularly the Blackfoot. Over the years he published several accounts of their religious practices, social life, and material culture. He began his study of Blackfoot mythology in 1903 and engaged Duvall, a young local man of mixed ancestry, to assist him. During the next eight years Duvall collected many stories that were sent to Wissler in New York, who edited them; they were published by the American Museum of Natural History. Of the approximately one hundred myths and legends collected by Duvall, twenty-three are Napi stories. This constitutes one of the largest bodies of literature relating to the trickster. Not only that, but Duvall was familiar with the nuances of the language and was able to offer concise and accurate renditions of the tales.

Christianus Uhlenbeck was an expert in the field of linguistics. In 1892 he was appointed chair of Sanskrit and comparative philology at the University of Amsterdam in Holland and seven years later became chair of Germanic languages at the University of Leiden, Germany. He focussed his attention on Indo-European, Basque, and American

Indian languages, but specialized in Blackfoot, writing a dictionary and grammar as well as publishing his language studies. His purpose in gathering Napi stories was to use them as part of his language research. His books on Blackfoot texts were published in both Blackfoot and English.

Jan de Josselin de Jong, Uhlenbeck's student, accompanied him to the Blackfeet Reservation in Montana in 1910. His primary goal was language studies, and the Napi stories appear to have been an afterthought. "I recorded those stories as a pastime during moments of rest," he wrote. He engaged an English-speaking informant, Walter Mountain Chief, and concedes that he had some difficulty conducting interviews in English. He wrote,

> No Indian, at least no old-fashioned Indian, is sufficiently conversant with English to render his ancient lore in it, nor does he possess any objective insight into his own inner life, enabling him to express his emotions, his beliefs, his very soul in the matter-of-fact idioms of the white man of his immediate environment . . . And who can render in English the spirit of this native lore, the deeply-felt solemnity pervading so many an Indian story, lending a wonderful charm to its short, childlike phrases without any literary artificiality?"[47]

During the twentieth century, members of the Blackfoot nation began to record their own Napi stories. Among them were people such as Jim White Bull, a Blood councillor who seemed to enjoy writing about the seamier side of Napi's adventures[48]; Joe Little Chief, a Siksika, whose accounts are handwritten and still unpublished[49]; Mike Mountain Horse, a Blood councillor who included Napi stories in his book *My People the Bloods*[50]; Darnell Davis Rides at the Door, a South Peigan, who compiled the booklet *Napi Stories*[51]; Cecil Black Plume, a Blood who provided stories to a newsletter of the Lethbridge Correctional Institute[52]; and Rosie Ayoungman, a Siksika whose stories were recorded on audiotape by Frances Fraser, who herself was the author of several Napi stories.[53] A number of South Peigan also contributed Napi stories to a Blackfeet cookbook.[54]

In a class by itself is Percy Bullchild's *The Sun Came Down: The History of the World as My Blackfeet Elders Told It*.[55] This book contains a strong element of Christian influence and attempts to meld many of the diverse and separate ritualistic and star myths into one cohesive picture of Blackfoot creation. Two leading figures are Mud Man and Rib Woman, who may be compared to Adam and Eve. While Bullchild tells Napi stories individually, he still tries to bring Napi into his orderly world. He writes,

> Creator Sun had always tried hard to find a special way to have his children go and live with good always. He had Napi to be with the people and taught them many things of goodness. Napi faltered at his job of teaching good, and he passed on from this world from his own foolishness. Then came Kut-toe-yis, a being from a clot of buffalo blood, to do away with the evil that he could find in the land, and which he did for Creator Sun.[56]

Bull Child's Napi stories depart noticeably from the norm. For example, he says that Crow Arrow, who figures in Blackfoot mythology, was really Napi and that Napi was put on earth to teach the children of Mother Earth and Father Sun how to live a sinless life. In short, the book is a wonderful literary piece but lacks the authenticity found in the writings of such people as Joe Little Chief, Darnell Rides at the Door, and Christianus Uhlenbeck.

Another author who is difficult to categorize is Frank Bird Linderman, who produced at least three books of legends, *Indian Why Stories* (1915), *Indian Old-Man Stories* (1920), and *Old Man Coyote* (1931), all reprinted in 1996 by Bison Books. Of these, the first deals primarily with the Blackfoot, the second with the Cree and Blackfoot, and the third with the Crow. Some of the tales in *Indian Why Stories* have familiar titles, such as "The Fire-Leggings" and "Why the Birch-Tree Wears the Slashes in Its Bark," but Linderman treats them as literary subjects and presents them in such a way that it is difficult to separate the story from the author's creative writing. They are highly entertaining but have limited value for serious study.

Similarly, the Napi stories and other tales collected by Sebastian Chumak appear to depart from the norm of stories recorded as they were told. *The Stonies of Alberta*, published in 1983, and *The Wisdom of the Blackfoot, the Bloods and the Peigans of Canada*, in 1988, are replete with trickster legends that in some cases appear to be derivative.[57] Not only that, but hero stories are incorrectly attributed to the trickster. Napi is also given credit for discovering the first horses,[58] creating Chief Mountain,[59] interfering with religious ceremonies,[60] and performing other questionable acts. The accounts themselves are accompanied by poems, sayings, or inspirational statements, presumably written by the editor. For example, "The deeper I enter the forest the louder the roaring of silence. Be joyous just sitting beside the river listening to the water speak."[61]

In his various stories, Chumak attributes the account of the bear losing his tail to Napi, yet Linderman tells the same story without the presence of the trickster.[62] Chumak also has accounts of two Indians fighting and Napi's hands fighting with each other, which appear to be found in no other source.[63] As a result, his information is treated with caution.

Numerous other references to Napi appear in various books and publications. Stories are found in collections of North American legends and other sources, as well as in modern adaptations of the Napi story, some equating Napi with Santa Claus.[64]

Napi stories still abound on the Blackfoot reserves. Some are remarkably close to those recorded over a century ago while others show the effects of modern life. Because of the influence of radio and television, Napi stories are seldom the source of an evening's entertainment, but when the occasion arises, elders still relate the stories as they were told to them. Schools sometimes invite elders into their classrooms to tell Napi and other culturally related stories.

In this study, few accounts have been taken from contemporary sources, primarily because of the richness of stories recorded decades ago, when the storytellers were unilingual and relatively uninfluenced by the outside world.

## CHRISTIANITY

One of the most intrusive features in the Napi myths has been the influence of Christianity. In particular, later Napi stories reveal attempts to find a common ground that goes beyond the creation story.

One story is an adaptation of a well-known star myth about seven brothers who were pursued by their mother and fled to the sky.[65] Neither Napi nor Jesus is part of the original story. In this version, the Sun was living on earth with a woman and they had a child called Napi. Two years later the woman asked for another child and was given a boy called The Maker. One day, while the Sun was out hunting, the woman slipped away from the camp and met her lover, who was a snake. Her actions were observed by their dog, which had the ability to speak. On the hunter's return, the dog told him about the affair and the Sun vowed revenge. He sent his wife away to bring in the deer he had killed, and when she was out of sight he killed the snake and called the two boys together.

"Your mother has a lot of power. I will give you this stone, this stick, this lump of dirt, and this drop of water. Take them and run for your lives. Your mother is not going to approve of me killing her serpent friend," he said.[66] He told them he was giving Napi and The Maker the power to create anything they liked.

A short time later, the angry mother poked her head inside the lodge and their father chopped it off. He then went into the sky and became the Sun, but the mother returned to life and began to pursue the boys, promising to kill them. When she got close, they dropped the stone and it became a range of mountains. When she got close again, they dropped the stick and it became a thick forest, then they dropped the lump of dirt, which became a deep canyon, and finally the water, which became a huge ocean. That ended the chase, and the mother went to the sky and became the moon. Napi and his brother now were on the east side of the ocean, but Napi became lonesome for the prairies. The Maker told him to close his eyes and make a wish, and he would be back home. He could stay there and create the Blackfoot people while The Maker would remain across the ocean where he would become Jesus.[67]

In another account, the Sun and Moon had two children, God and Napi. The two boys kept asking their parents for things, until God asked his father for daylight. However, the Moon protested and said she would kill the boy if his father acceded to his wish. One day, the Moon slipped away to meet her lover, a snake, but when the Sun learned of it he killed the serpent. When the Moon tried to kill her husband and two children the Sun cut her head off. But then her head began to pursue them. As with the previous story, the boys put up barriers, the last being the ocean. The head tried to leap over it but fell into the water and perished.

As the two boys stood on the east side of the ocean, God decided to join his father, the Sun, in the sky and turned Napi into a white swan. He then created a man and woman, placing the man on the right wing of the swan and the woman on the left. Carrying them, Napi returned home where he created birds, animals, trees, and other objects of nature, and in the end turned himself into a pine tree.[68]

A third variation has an even closer, albeit confused, association with Christianity. In this story are Napi and Jesus. Napi made the first people, and that generation was led by Holy Child, then by Bullet Hawk. During this time Jesus was crucified by the Holy Ghost, who took the form of a dove, and his blood was used for baptism. In three days he ascended into Heaven. After this happened, the Sun sent down an angel in the form of a crow that told Bullet Hawk to kill the dove, take its heart, and sacrifice it on an altar. From then on, whenever they had a ceremony, the dove's blood was used as incense. And from that time on, people had blood inside them.[69] (At this point, the storyteller included Scar Face and the Woman married the Morning Star, but these two figures are the subject of separate myths that do not include Napi.[70]) Meanwhile, Napi, who also was the devil, was seen by his dog having intercourse with a woman. When the dog tried to tell others about it, Napi rubbed manure in its mouth and the dog lost the ability to speak. From that time on, people and animals could no longer understand each other.

The final story has Napi competing with the Great Spirit where whole mountains were moved. Also, a man and woman were created, and the Great Spirit said to Napi, "I will make a big cross for you to carry." Napi refused and said, "You make another man so that he can carry it." The Great Spirit created a white man and gave him the cross, but after a while he got tired, so he was sent off alone in the wilderness as a wanderer. Meanwhile, the man and woman travelled south to Mexico where they tried to build a mountain to reach the sky but they got mixed up with other people and when they came down, they all spoke different languages.[71] In this short account, Jesus, his crucifixion, and the Tower of Babel are all part of a Napi story.

In these instances, the Christian content was not applied to an existing Napi story but to a star or ritualistic myth. In them, Napi was parachuted in as the devil or as someone who was a counterpart or foil to Jesus. The result was an origin tale that created a convenient place for Napi in the teachings of Christianity. According to Horatio Hale in 1887,

> This modern shaping of the Blackfoot mythological stories is also apparent in the account of the making of the first woman and man from the ribs of Napi. This portion of the creation myth, which does not appear in the version furnished to me by Father Lacombe, is evidently a novel feature, derived very recently from the missionary teachings.[72]

## STORYTELLING

There is a tradition that the myths were told in sequence.[73] De Jong commented, "As regards the texts it should in the first place be noted that they are to be considered as forming one continuous series."[74] This is implied in the storytelling of Uhlenbeck and de Jong, who usually begin a new story with a sentence such as "There he went again,"[75] "There was the Old Man, he was travelling about again,"[76] or "He went along again, the Old Man."[77]

While de Jong and Uhlenbeck placed their myths in a particular order, many stories are not included in their list. I have therefore presented the myths in an order that makes sense to me, but may not have been the way a Blackfoot storyteller saw it. He might have had reasons for following a sequence that any contemporary Blackfoot or non-Indian might find unfathomable. Generally speaking, the myths in this book appear in this sequence: the creation of the earth, creation of creatures, their adventures, creation of the first woman, creation of men and women, their adventures, arrangement for the first marriages, Napi turning himself into a pine tree, and what came later. Scattered among them are stories that do not fit into any neat category.

I have looked at anywhere from three to a dozen versions of each myth. In presenting them, I have followed the most frequent version, plus added features that may exist in one legend but not in others. The results, I feel, are well-rounded stories that adhere to the most accepted versions of the myth but in a more extended form. For example, when Napi tosses his eyes so that they stick to a tree, there is a mention of dead trees, willows, straight trees, white trees, and tree branches. Of these, dead trees are most frequently mentioned and are used in the story. On the other hand, the willows that were said to hold Napi's eyes we recognize today as pussywillows.

The stories from various Blackfoot informants show considerable variation in detail, but this is to be expected. An elderly Blood, in discussing the matter, pulled a common ragweed from the ground and stated, "The parts of this weed all branch from the stem. They go different ways, but all come from the same root. So it is with the different versions of a myth."[78]

Variations in the myths are affirmed by Darnell Rides at the Door, who states, "Napi stories have been passed down from generation to generation in the Blackfeet Nation up until today. Each family has their own interpretation of the various Napi stories, but in the final analysis each story has a common moral in the ending."[79] Variations may occur because of the speaker's style of storytelling, the person may have forgotten details of the story, or they have added their own embellishments. Outside influences, such as scepticism about the supernatural brought about by modern education or the sensitivity regarding a discussion of sexual acts, might also affect the structure and content of a story. Wissler and Duvall addressed this problem of consistency in their own way. They state,

Each narrator has his own version, in the telling of which he is usually consistent; and, while the main features of the myths are the same for all, the minor differences are so great that extreme accuracy of detail with one individual would avail little. The method pursued here with the most important myths was to discuss them with different individuals, so as to form an opinion as to the most common arrangement of incidents; a statement of such opinions being given as footnotes . . . [T]o say that any one version of those myths is correct would be preposterous, because they have not now, and probably never did have an absolutely fixed form. The only rational criterion seems to be the approximate form in which the myth is most often encountered.[80]

## COMPARATIVE DATA

Napi was not alone as a trickster. Other similar creatures were known to Indigenous people all across North America and throughout the world. Whether it was Raven on the West Coast, Bluebird in the Southwest, Rabbit in the Southeast, or Nanabush with the Algonkian in the East, they all shared the same characteristics. As they travelled they created the landscapes around them and interacted with creatures they met—sometimes humorously and sometimes tragically. Their stories are a rich part of the folklore of Indigenous North America.

One of the most common tricksters was Coyote, who figures in the mythology of many Indigenous peoples, including the Sioux, Apache, Cheyenne, and Salish. Then there was Old Man Coyote with the Pawnee, Kootenay, and Crow, as well as Inktomi among the Assiniboine and Sioux, and Wasakushak with the Cree. Not only did these and other tribes have tricksters, but they often shared the same stories. Variations of Napi myths can be found all across North America.

In most of these stories, the trickster is an animal, such as a coyote or raven, that interacts with other animals. There are also stories where the form of the trickster involved is not specified, but the reader might assume it is human. Other stories belie this designation. For example, the Blackfoot story of Napi raping and killing a girl tells of him having to jump across a creek to prove his innocence. However, he gives his weighty penis to a chickadee that fails to make the jump. One must ask: if the camp was made up of humans, what was a chickadee doing there? If the camp was made up of animals, then the tale would make sense.

Also, when he made people, if Napi was in human form and he made them after his own image, there would have been no need for him to experiment. Yet in one account he began by giving men paws instead of feet,[81] while in another, women had eyes and mouths placed vertically, had no noses, long ears, three fingers on each hand, and three toes on each foot.[82] After experimenting, he finally brought them to their final form. Folklorist Barry Lopez was so convinced that Napi was an animal that when reprinting stories by George Bird Grinnell, he incorrectly changed the name in the text from "Napi" to "Coyote."[83] A reasonable assumption, however, is that the Blackfoot borrowed some stories from other tribes where the exploits were those of the animal Coyote. When the Blackfoot adopted these tales, they were attributed to the human-like Napi but were not a perfect fit.

One of the most intriguing Napi stories, in which he is chased by a rock, is found in varying forms among a number of North American tribes. In the Blackfoot account, which we have already mentioned, Napi loans his blanket to a rock then takes it back. The rock pursues him and various animals try to stop it but fail. At last two nighthawks fart on the rock and break it in two. Napi then punishes them for spoiling his fun and disfigures their babies.

A Pawnee story is similar, except Old Man Coyote gives the rock a knife and takes it back. As in the Blackfoot story, while he is being pursued, nighthawks peck at the rock until it is reduced to pebbles, and then Old Man Coyote disfigures the nighthawks' babies. But this is not the end of the Pawnee story. In it, the angry nighthawks reassemble the rock, which then attacks Old Man Coyote and flattens him. In a Gros Ventre version, Nix'ant (Coyote) hides under a rock to escape a little bird with a big arrow (a separate Napi story) and is trapped. Nighthawks fart on the rock and break it. Nix'ant, like Napi, then disfigures the birds.[84]

A Sioux legend tells of Coyote giving his blanket to a rock and then taking it back. The rock pursues him, even across a deep river, finally catches him, and then flattens him. A rancher takes him home to use as a rug, but he jumps up and runs away.[85] In the Cheyenne account, Coyote defecates and urinates on a rock and scratches it like a dog. The angry rock pursues him through hills and forests with various animals trying to stop him. At last the rock is broken and is stopped. Coyote then steals some beads from another rock and it also pursues him. Finally, nighthawks shout at the rock and it breaks into pieces.[86] Similarly, in an Apache story, Coyote defecates and urinates on a rock. It pursues him, but instead of being flattened, Coyote is forced to lick the rock clean.[87] An Assiniboine legend tells of the rock asking Inktomi for a gift but is refused. The rock then traps him for four days. Finally, some birds blow on the rock until it shatters.[88] In the Stoney Nakoda variation, Inktomi offers to race a rock. It pursues him and flattens him "like a buffalo chip."[89] Four days later, Coyote jumps on Inktomi's body, reviving him.

In a Coeur d'Alene story, a rock is angry and destroying everything, so the birds call upon trickster Coyote to save them. He teases the rock until it chases him. As it bounces up and down, it creates mountains, such as Mount Spokane, then becomes blue from rolling through patches of huckleberries. Finally, Coyote lures it over a cliff where it falls into Coeur d'Alene Lake and turns the water blue.[90]

In all these accounts, the Blackfoot story is the only one where the landscape supports the story of a rolling rock. The area from the Blood Reserve and 150 kilometres north of the town of Okotoks contains a string of glacial erratics. Some as large as bungalows, these rocks fit perfectly into the story of Napi being chased and the big rock having portions of it chipped away by nighthawks and eventually split in two. One huge rock just southwest of the town of Okotoks is split in two, just like in the story. This is one of the few instances where one can conclude, with some assurance, that the legend had its origin among the Blackfoot and then spread to other tribes in North America, all the way south to the Apache.

Two other stories may also have originated with the Blackfoot, or at least were of great antiquity in the tribe. One is the account of a bobcat stealing Napi's roasted prairie dogs and the other is the coyote's theft of his elk meat. In the first story, the name of the bobcat, Nap-iyo, is translated as Old Man Greasy Stepping, based upon the legend. The name for nighthawk, *pisto*, or fart, is also based on a Napi story. To have become a part of the tribe's language would support the idea of antiquity or perhaps origin. With most stories, however, it is difficult if not impossible to conclusively identify the tribe of origin.

The story of the flood is quite common across North America. As early as 1634, Paul le Jeune spoke of native beliefs in a great flood[91] and in 1724, Joseph François Lafitau, a Jesuit who took the Bible literally, wrote, "the Indians all have some knowledge of the flood which, since it was universal as it is reasonable to conclude from the teaching of our faith about it, was an event so singular and remarkable that vestiges of it must necessarily remain in [the mythology] of all nations."[92] The details of events after the flood vary from the trickster being on a raft or canoe to being on top of a mountain. Various creatures were sent into the water for soil; the successful one was a turtle, duck, or helldiver, but the most frequently mentioned was the muskrat. When the trickster received the soil, he either rolled it or blew on it to create the earth. In this way, according to the Blackfoot, his world was created.

Many trickster adventures among various tribes are similar to each other and all stress his voracious appetite, exceptional sexual abilities, and ability to fool other creatures or be fooled by them. The trickster's character is summed up by Paul Radin:

> Trickster is at one and the same time creator and destroyer, giver and negator, he who dupes others and who is always duped himself. He wills nothing consciously. At all times he is constrained to behave as he does from impulses over which he has no control. He knows neither good nor evil yet he is responsible for both. He possesses no value, moral or social, is at the mercy of his passions and appetites, yet through his actions all values come into being. But not only he, so our myth tells us, possesses these traits.[93]

## THE PSYCHOLOGY OF TRICKSTERS

Trickster stories have proven to be fertile ground for many psychologists, anthropologists, and sociologists, including Claude Lévi-Strauss, Carl Jung, and Sigmund Freud. Lévi-Strauss says the trickster is a feature of myths that allow cultures to explain certain "technological and economic conditions linked with the natural environment."[94] Jung says that tricksters reflect an archetype buried in the mind of all human beings,[95] while Freud develops the hypothesis that myths are projective systems that reflect sexual impulses repressed during early childhood.[96] Barbara Babcock-Abrahams states that the trickster stories represent the "fundamental contradiction . . . between individual and society."[97] Esther S. Goldfrank, speaking of the Blackfoot, says that in a society where the institutions encouraged an idealization of the father, Napi "offered a vigorous and uncensored release for the son's repressed feelings of aggression."[98]

Michael Carroll considers the trickster to be "simultaneously portrayed as a selfish buffoon and as the culture-hero who makes human society possible"—"'selfish' because so much of the trickster's energy is oriented toward the gratification of his enormous appetites for food and sex, and 'buffoon' because the elaborate deceits that the trickster devises in order to satisfy these appetites so often backfire and leave the trickster looking incredibly foolish."[99] At the same time, he is also a culture hero, "responsible for creating the conditions that allowed for the development of human civilization."[100]

In North America, tricksters have been grouped into five categories, with all but one of these being associated with animals. These are the Coyote, Raven, Hare, Spider, and Napi. Indigenous peoples that have the Coyote, or Old Man Coyote, as their trickster include the Apache, Crow, Shoshone, Ktunaxa (Kootenai), Mandan, Pawnee, Caddo, Coeur d'Alene, Kalapuya, Hidatsa, Shuswap, Cochiti, and Taos Pueblo. The Raven is found mostly among coastal tribes—the Haida, Heiltsuk, Tsimshian, Tsilhqot'in, and Tlingit. The Hare is a trickster among the Cree, Natchez, Chippewa, Alabama, Menominee, Mississauga, Hitchiti, and Coushatta (Koasati). Spider, or Inktomi, is found among the Sioux, Assiniboine, Stoney Nakoda, Winnebago, Ponca, Omaha, Arapaho,

Cheyenne, and Gros Ventre. Only the Blackfoot have as their trickster a human, or human-like figure, in Napi, the Old Man.

How a mythological figure can be both a fool and a hero has been the subject of discussion for many years. In 1896, Daniel Brinton theorized that the trickster started out as a cultural hero who was debased and degraded over time.[101] Conversely, in 1898, Franz Boas believed that the hero figure initially developed among the more advanced tribes, replacing the buffoon.[102] Neither of these arguments have stood the test of time. Similarly, the contention that the trickster was less important to tribes that followed an agricultural way of life has not been proven.[103]

Freud's belief was that unless human beings inhibit their instinctual desire for sexual pleasure, orderly social life would be impossible.[104] Carroll expands on this point, saying that people want both gratification of their impulses and the orderly development of civilization. The first part of this is reflected in the selfish buffoon nature of the trickster. If his desires were unchecked, it would lead to the destruction of a culture. The second is indicated by the trickster's role as a creator or cultural hero.[105]

Carroll believes it is important to realize that the trickster is basically a loner. Levern says, "He always travelled, as he had no house, and he was always alone."[106] Animals with whom he is identified, such as coyotes, ravens, hares, and spiders, Carroll points out, do not live in colonies with members of their own species but remain apart. Thus, their unsavoury habits are not shared by society as a whole. Napi, like other tricksters, seldom interacted with other creatures except through trickery. This means that people can look at his antics but not identify personally with them, as they are the actions of a loner, someone outside of society.

The psychology of the trickster has been examined inside and out, backwards and forwards, and up and down. With the knowing nods of great thinkers, scholars believe they understand him. Native people, on the other hand, simply accept the trickster for what he is—an anomaly that was never taken too seriously.

# *Napi Stories*

---

Around the turn of the twentieth century, Blackfoot people told these stories to anthropologists, missionaries, and other interested people. They were then transcribed into various manuscripts and publications. The stories on the following pages bring together elements from different sources, and the dialogue is drawn directly from these sources. The sources are indicated in an endnote at the conclusion of each story.

Variations are explored in an annotation.

# Creation

There was water everywhere as far as the eye could see. The only object to be seen was a small raft, drifting aimlessly, and on it were five creatures—a muskrat, a beaver, an otter, a duck, and a human-like character known to all as Napi, the Old Man. He wasn't really old, he was ageless, an object of creation.

Napi became impatient sitting on the raft, so he turned to the animals and said, "My younger brothers, dive in and try to bring back some earth." The first to dive was the beaver. It plunged into the water and was gone a long time, but finally bobbed to the surface, drowned. Napi sent the otter into the water, but it too could not reach the land beneath the sea and died. Then came the duck, but the water was so deep that he drowned like the others. As the muskrat was the only animal left, Napi turned to him and said, "You must dive to the bottom of the water and bring up some earth."

The animal disappeared into the water and was gone longer than the other three, but finally it too bobbed to the surface, dead. As it lay on its back, all four feet in the air, Napi noticed a little piece of mud clinging to one of its claws. He took it, rolled it in his hands, and watched as it grew larger and larger. Finally, it was too big for him to hold and it fell onto the raft, and when the raft was too small, the huge ball fell into the water and continued to grow. Napi watched in satisfaction as the earth spread in all directions to the horizon; he then brought the four animals back to life and sent them scampering off into the new world.

Napi set out from the south[107] to explore the land and to fix it the way he wanted. He spread grass over the prairie and marked where rivers should run. In some instances their courses were smooth, but in other places he created cascades and waterfalls. Travelling north, he made the Teton River, then rested for a while. When he continued his journey he tripped over a knoll and fell to his knees. "You are a bad thing to be stumbling against," he said, so he made two large buttes there and called them the Knees.[108] He created the mountains, including a range that extended eastward across the prairies from Chief Mountain to the Sweetgrass Hills. He made foothills and forests, small trees and bushes, and caused roots and berries to grow. There was one place for wild turnips, another for chokecherries, and ones for bull berries and saskatoons. He then created all kinds of birds and animals that could live off the land.

He put the bighorn sheep on the prairie, where he noticed it moved awkwardly. He took it up into the hills and let it go among the rocks. It skipped along cliffs and climbed easily up to places other animals were afraid to go. Old Man said the bighorn was fit for this place, for the mountains and the rough country. While he was in the mountains Napi made the antelope, and turned it loose to see how it performed. The little animal ran so fast that it fell over some rocks and hurt itself. Napi saw that this would not do, so he took it down to the prairie and set it free there, where it ran away fast and gracefully. He said to it, "This is the place that suits you." He made the Milk River Ridge, the Belly River, the Old Man, and the Bow River. North of the Bow he lay down to rest and marked the place with stones to the shape of his body, arms, legs, and penis. Near the end of his journey he lay down on the west bank of the Red Deer River, again marking the site.

Meanwhile, across the mountains lived another supernatural person, Mountain Man, who had created objects there. The two met on the upper waters of the Oldman River, where they started playing the wheel and arrow game and betting on the outcome. One person threw a small hoop, and as it rolled along, the other followed it, holding an arrow in his hand. Just before the wheel fell, he tossed the arrow so that the point fell under it. The winner was declared based upon the position of the arrow.

First they wagered over who would control the east–west mountain ranges. Napi lost, and the Mountain Man took all the mountains out of the prairies except those at the far eastern end where he left the Sweetgrass Hills, Bears Paw Mountains, and Wolf Mountain. Next they played for the buffalo herds. This time Napi threw the winning arrow and took control of the herds. That is why there are no buffalo west of the Rockies.[109]

Another supernatural figure came down from the north and began to gamble with them. Napi, who was watching the game, bet his hair that the Northern Man would lose, while the Mountain Man bet some of his mountains. With a throw of the arrow, the Northern Man won and took the mountains and placed them in the north. He was about to take Napi's scalp when the Mountain Man stopped him.

"No," he said, "this is the creator; do not touch his hair but take mine." So the Northern Man took the Mountain Man's scalp.

"Go home now with your trophy," Napi told the Mountain Man, "then blacken your face and dance." This is how scalping came to be.

Napi wandered through his new land, but he soon became bored. He was bored very easily. And he was lonely. At last he sat down beside a river and decided to create some companions. Starting with a woman, he shaped her body in clay:

> He had given her eyes but it so happened that the eyes were placed vertically, as was the mouth. There was no nose and the ears were too long. There were eight teeth in all, four on each side. Then the Old Man made her fingers but there were only three and three toes.[110]

Tired from the exertion, Napi lay down and took a nap and in a dream he saw how the woman should be made. When he awoke, he chewed the ears off the clay figure, added fingers, changed the position of the eyes and mouth, added a nose, and increased the number of teeth. When he was finished, he made a child in a similar form. He covered them up and came back a day later to examine them. They had changed a little. The second morning, he could see more changes and on the third day even more. On the fourth morning, he looked at the figures and told them to get up and walk. They did so, and he said to them, "You must be people."

A short time later, Napi was standing by a river when the woman came up to him and asked, "How is it? Will we always live; will there be no end to it?"

"I never thought of that," replied Napi. "We'll have to decide it. I'll take this buffalo chip and throw it in the river. If it floats, when people die, in four days they will become alive again; they will die for only four days. But if it sinks, there will be an end to them."

Napi threw the buffalo chip into the river and it floated.

But the woman picked up a stone and said, "No, if this stone goes to the bottom of the water, people will die forever and those who are dead will be mourned." She threw the stone into the water and it sank to the bottom. The woman said, "When someone dies, people will weep and be very sad."

"There," said Napi, "you have chosen. There will be an end to them."

A short time later the child died and the woman went into mourning. She went to Napi and begged him to change the rules, to throw the buffalo chip into the water. "Not so," said Napi. "What is made law must be law. We will undo nothing that we have done. The child is dead; it cannot be changed. People will have to die."

Napi and the woman discussed other laws that needed to be considered. Napi believed that people should eat the bark of trees and suck the sap from its trunks. "The food will not be swallowed," said Napi, "and in that way it will not be destroyed." No, said the woman, people will eat animals, not bark.

Then, said Napi, "The buffalo, the mountain goats, all the birds, and the animals which walk on the earth will be revived at the end of four days." No, replied the woman, they will die forever.

Napi suggested that the buffalo and other animals be tame so that men could easily kill them. The woman disagreed. "That will make a man very lazy," she said. "Man should go out and work hard for his living and food."

"The women are to tan the hides," continued Napi. "When they do this, they are to rub brains on them to make them soft; they are to scrape them well with scraping-tools, etc. But all this they are to do very quickly, for it will not be very hard work."

"No, I will not agree to this," said the woman. "They must tan the hide in the way you say; but it must be made very hard work, and take a long time, so that the good workers may be found out."

Napi suggested that wood be used for making fires but it would not be consumed and could be used over and over again. "No," argued the woman, "people will have to look for wood every day."

Napi tried again. Even in the winter, there should be wild fruit, he said. No, replied the woman, in winter they should fall from their branches. And so it went, and each time the future was considered, the woman had the final choice.[111]

After the death of the child, the woman left the camp and went to live alone. Now that Napi had learned how to make people, he began creating men, giving them life and sending them off into the prairies. Some time later while travelling about, he found that they were naked and unable to care for themselves. He showed them roots and berries and told them which ones they could eat. He showed them different plants, telling them the ones that were good to eat and those that could be used for medicine.

At this time the men were hiding in the mountains, and when Napi asked them why, they said they were afraid of the buffalo. At that time these were huge black animals with long ears and armed with weapons. The men pointed out some of the people who had been attacked by the buffalo. They were lying dead, torn to pieces, and partly consumed by buffalo. Napi saw that this would not do and vowed to change it, so that the people would eat the buffalo instead.

He asked the men why they did nothing to the buffalo. They said they did not know what to do because they had no way to kill the animals, while the buffalo were armed. Napi said, "That isn't hard." He said he would make them a weapon.

He cut some saskatoon berry shoots and peeled the bark off. He found a larger piece of wood, flattened it, and tied a sinew cord to it to make a bow. He then caught a bird and from its wing took feathers that he split and tied to the arrow. At first he used four feathers, but the arrow missed its mark and did not fly well. He then tried three feathers and found these were much better. Next he needed a sharp point, so he went out and began to break sharp pieces off the stones. He tried them and found that the black flint stones were the sharpest and made the best arrow points and knife blades.

He taught the men how to shoot and to aim at the heart of the buffalo. When they acquired some skill, he told them to make bows and arrows of their own and to practice with them. When they were ready, he led them out from the mountains to a place where the buffalo had built an impoundment that they used to drive men over a cliff for food. Two rows of stone piles were laid out in ever-narrowing lines, converging at the edge of a cliff. While some of the buffalo were hiding behind the stone piles, Napi changed himself into a buffalo calf and sought out the two bulls who were in charge of the drive. He led them to the men where they were rounded up and driven towards the empoundment. As the men ran towards the cliff, the buffalo behind the stone piles jumped up and roared at them. The men ran faster and faster with the buffalo in pursuit but at the last moment they veered to one side and the buffalo went over the cliff instead of them. Armed with their bows and arrows, the men slaughtered the animals until only two bulls and a few cows escaped. These were the ancestors of all the buffalo that came later.

The men used their flint knives to butcher the buffalo, but Napi warned them it was not healthy to eat the meat raw. He gathered some dry wood and showed them how to make a fire and cook the meat. He also told them that the spirits of various animals could be a guide to them. "You may go to sleep, and get power," he said. "Something will come to you in your dream that will help you. Whatever these animals tell you to do, you must obey them as they appear to you in your sleep. Be guided by them. . . . It may be by the eagles, perhaps by the buffalo, or by the bears. Whatever animal answers your prayers, you must listen to him."

While he was with the men, Napi took a white stone, sat in on a buffalo trail, then gave four shouts, and transformed it into a white buffalo. "You will be very scarce," he told the animal. He also made a fine beaver-haired buffalo the same way. Napi then warned the men about eating these special creatures. "If you eat the meat of a white or beaver-haired buffalo," he said, "you will be turned into a spotted person." He added, "Whoever kills one of these rare animals must not keep its skin long but he must give it to the Sun, with a great feast to all people."

After this meeting, Napi began to travel north to visit the land he had created. The serious work of creation behind him, he was now ready for a little fun.[112]

........................................................................................

*The creatures in the raft at the beginning of the story vary. Wissler and Duvall say they were an otter, a beaver, and a duck. Hale says they were an otter, a beaver, a muskrat, and a badger. Levern says an otter, a beaver, a muskrat, and an osprey, while Grinnell says an otter, a beaver, a muskrat, and a loon. Both Mountain Horse and Fraser Taylor say it was only a muskrat. And Maclean says a fish, a frog, a lizard, and a turtle.*

*In Christian-influenced versions of the creation of life from mud, Napi breathes on the mud four times to bring them to life, while some say that the woman was formed from Napi's lower rib.*

*A stone marker just south of Crowfoot siding, where stones are laid in the shape of a man, indicates the place north of the Bow where Napi lay down to rest.*

*The place where Napi and the others had gambled was marked with stones, and in later years some Blackfoot went there to play the wheel and arrow game. Napi joined them and bet his robe and moccasins. When he lost he took them off, but the robe immediately turned into back fat and the moccasins into buffalo tongues. The gamblers had no use for these objects, so they gave them back. Napi put them back on and again they became a robe and moccasins. This way, Napi was able to play again and again, always with the same result.*

*An addition to the story, recorded by R.N. Wilson, involves an explanation for why fat and meat are always on the same place on a buffalo. At the point in the story when the buffalo jumped up and roared, Wilson says, "A cow near the pound was at this time sitting down and about to paint her face and had in her 'hand' a piece of fat for the purpose. At the alarm she stuck the fat between her toes and caught up a piece of meat and put it under her arm and made off."[113]*

# Napi, the Elk, and the Lame Coyote

Napi was wandering along Sheep Creek in the late evening when he saw some elk playing follow the leader and having great fun. After he had watched them for a while, he started crying until the elk leader sent someone to find out what was wrong. "I wish I could do like them," said Napi.

When the leader learned the reason for his unhappiness, the elk said, "Well, come and have some fun with us." He added, "We are leading each other." He then demonstrated how he took a burning stick and tossed it over a shallow cliff. The elk, in turn, followed the fire brand and landed safely on the sandy bottom.

Meanwhile, Napi looked around until he found a high cliff then told the elk he wanted his turn as leader. Taking the fire brand, he led them around for a while, jumping over stones, bushes, and even little gullies until it was night, all the while leading them towards the steep precipice. When they arrived, he jumped into the darkness, the fire showing the way. He was knocked out for a few minutes by the fall, and when he woke up he called for the elk to follow him.

"No," said the elk, "we might hurt ourselves."

"Oh," responded Napi, "it is nice and soft here, and I had to sleep a while."

So, one at a time, the elk jumped and each was killed on the rocks below. Finally, there was only one elk left, a cow heavy with calf. "They have all jumped but you," said Old Man. "Come on, you will like it."

But the cow answered, "Take pity on me. I am very heavy, and I am afraid to jump."

"Go away, then," said Old Man, "go and live. Then some day there will be plenty of elk again."

Napi hauled the carcasses to a handy spot where he could build a shelter. This done, he skinned the animals, cut up the meat, and broke the bones to boil for soup. He also placed the elk tongues on poles to keep them away from mice.

While he was in his shelter cooking some fat for grease, a coyote came by, begging for a little food. The animal was lame, one leg tied up with a strip of hide,[114] and around his neck he wore a beautiful necklace decorated with a large shell. Napi refused to feed the beggar and threatened to hit him over the head with his penis if he didn't leave. When the coyote persisted, Napi said he would feed him in exchange for his necklace.

"No," answered the coyote. "This is my holy shell given to me by an old Coyote so I can have good luck and long life."

Napi then suggested that they have a race. If the coyote won, Napi would feed him; if he lost, he had to give up the necklace.

"Well," said Coyote, "I'm hurt. I can't run."

"That makes no difference, run anyway."

"Well," said the coyote, "I will run for a short distance."

"No. You have to run a long distance."

At last the coyote agreed, but because of his bad leg he asked that they walk some distance from the camp before starting. When they reached a ridge, the coyote complained it was still too far. Believing he could easily win the match over a lame coyote, Napi agreed to go to the next ridge, out of sight of the camp, and there the race began. Coyote started out very slowly from the starting place and kept crying for Napi to wait for him. When at last they reached the turning point, the coyote threw off his strap and disappeared quickly down the trail towards the camp.

Realizing he had been tricked, Napi cried out to the rapidly disappearing animal, "Little brother, leave some meat for me!"

But the coyote paid no attention; as he ran, he howled four times, calling for all the animals to come to a feast. And they came. There were coyotes, wolves, bears, badgers, foxes, kit foxes, wild cats, weasels, and even mice. The coyote directed his relatives to take the choicest pieces of meat, the bears to take the fat, and the mice he sent up the poles to eat the tongues. The others feasted on the haunches, ribs, and other parts of the elk. The rabbits were late and found only some fat to grease their shoulders. That is why the shoulders are the only place one can find fat on rabbits today.

When Napi got back to the camp, he saw that all his food was gone. Looking up, he said, "Oh, well, I still have my flags." But when he brought the tongues down, he found they were hollow. The mice had eaten all the insides, leaving only the skins. So the Old Man starved again.[115]

. . . . . . . . . . . . . . . . . . . . . . . . . . . . . . . . . . . . . . . . . . . . . . . . . . . . . . . . . . . . . . . . . . . . . . . . . . . . . . . . . . . . . . . . . . . . . . . . .

*In some versions, the animal that is tricked is not an elk but a deer or antelope. According to informants, this was one of Napi's first adventures, or misadventures, with animals. His impetus for tricking the elk was one of hunger, a theme that persists through his various stories. One of the earliest versions, recorded by Wilson in the early 1890s, is more detailed than the others and deals with Napi having adventures with three coyotes (or wolves), not just one, as in later accounts. The outcome, however, is generally the same. All versions include the preservation of the species, Napi being outsmarted, the mice being triumphant, and Napi generally being resigned to the loss of food. "Save me some of the meat!" cries Napi to the rapidly disappearing coyote, a comment sure to amuse the story's listeners.*

*The tale is one of several that have a specific geographical location. According to both Wilson and Maclean, the killing of the elk occurred on the banks of Sheep Creek while the pilfering of Napi's food happened on Tongue Creek (Matsin-awastam, Tongue Flag), a site about forty kilometres south of Calgary. The creek is named for the Napi incident.*

*A similar version of this story is told by the Stoney Nakoda, except the elk parade is not included and the creatures killed were grouse and not elk.[116]*

# The Rock

❋

Old Man was travelling about with his younger brother, Kit Fox. They went north until they reached the Bow River, where Napi lay down and had a nap. Stones marked this place that can still be seen today. The pair wandered up the Bow River to the mountains, where they came to a hill. Just for fun, Napi slid down the slope, bringing a great number of stones with him. This bank of shale can be seen today near Morley. At this point, according to White Bull, the pair turned south.

They crossed all the rivers south from Bow River—Elbow River, Sheep River, Tongue River, Highwood River, Mosquito Creek, Willow Creek, and Old Man River. By the time they crossed the Kootenay [Waterton] River, it was one of the hottest days in mid-summer. Tired, Napi lay down in the shade of a big rock and went to sleep. When he woke up he said to Kit Fox, "A day like this, men don't need any clothes. Oh, well, I guess I'll leave my robe with this rock. I'll let him have it for a present. I don't need it any more. All right, Mr. Big Rock, you can have my robe."

Napi and Kit Fox went on, and as they crossed a hill they heard a loud thundering noise. Looking back, they saw a dark rain cloud with flashing lightning and rolling thunder coming towards them. "Run back," Napi told his younger brother. "Tell the rock that I want to use his robe just for the rain." The fox ran back but the rock would not surrender it.

"No," said the rock. "Once you have given me your robe for a present, you must not take it back from me."

Kit Fox delivered the message, but as the storm came closer Napi sent him back a second time. "Run back again," he urged his companion. "Tell him, I want to use it just for the rain."

But the rock refused. "I will not give it to him. He has already given it to me." On the third try, the rock said, "What has been given to big rocks, that is never taken back from them." Four times Napi sent Kit Fox to get the robe but each time the rock refused.

Finally, Napi ran back to the rock himself and said angrily, "After all these years in the past you have been sitting here without a robe. What did you do for rain and snow then?" He snatched the robe from the rock and stalked off.

After the rainstorm, Napi was worried about the argument, and four times he sent Kit Fox back to see if the rock was still where they had left it. Reassured that it had not moved, Napi continued his journey. A short time later he heard rumbling behind him. Fearing another thunderstorm, Napi sent his little brother to see if it was coming their way. But it was

not a storm. Kit Fox came running down the ridge crying, "The stone is coming after us." Looking back, Napi saw Kit Fox had spoken the truth. The huge rock was rolling towards them, so they both ran for their lives.

The younger brother was faster than Napi, so from time to time he would run back and look. "He keeps getting closer to us!" he shouted.

After they had been running for a long time, Kit Fox became tired, so he dived into a badger hole, but it was so small that he was stuck with his rear end sticking out. The rock came up and rolled right over him, pushing him inside and sealing up the hole.

As he ran, Napi saw two young buffalo bulls and shouted to them, "Quick, my friends, stop this rock or it will kill me!" The bulls rushed at the rock, but it crushed them both under its mighty weight. A little farther on, Napi met two bears and shouted for help, but they suffered the same fate as the buffalo.

Said Napi to himself, "I must run for my life. I don't want to die so soon. I'm still a young man yet." He went across the Belly River and west

past the Belly Buttes when he heard two nighthawks, Pistox, singing in the air. Napi looked up and shouted, "Fly down to me, my brothers. I need your help! Hurry! Hurry!"

"What's wrong with you, brother?" asked one nighthawk. "You look like somebody's been chasing you all over the country."

The other bird said, "All right, brother Napi, don't worry. Just take an easy run. We'll fix the big rock."

Responded Napi, "If you save me, you will get your reward from me."

Closing in on the big rock, the nighthawks swooped down on it, farting at it again and again. Each time the flatulence struck, it caused a piece to come flying off the stone. Even today, one can see these chunks of rock extending all the way north from the Waterton River to the Highwood. At last one of the nighthawks made a spectacular dive and its fart split the rock in two. It could roll no further and came to rest beside a small creek. Thus the creek is named Oqkotoqseetuqta (the Rock Creek, or Stony Creek), although today it is known as Sheep Creek.

Napi had been saved, so he went on his way in good spirits. Alongside the river he came to a nest of baby nighthawks and asked them, "Where are your parents?"

"Out," they said, "getting food for us."

"Oh, I know your parents. What business did they have to come and spoil my play with the rock out there on the prairie? Who told them to break up the rock when I was having so much fun?"

Saying that, Napi put his fingers into each bird's mouth and stretched it wide. Then, with a stone, he hammered each one's mouth until all their beaks were crooked. "That is how you will always look," he said, and even today the nighthawks have big mouths and crooked beaks.

Later, when the parents came home they saw the children's beaks were bloody. "You have been eating," they said. "Where did you get the meat that made your mouths bloody?" When they explained what Napi had done to them, the parents flew off in search of him. When they found him they dived on him again and again, farting each time and knocking off a piece of his robe. Napi ran for his life, but the birds continued to pursue him until he jumped into a nearby lake and the last of his robe was blown away. Napi tried to stay under the water, but each time he came up for air, one of the nighthawks shot him in the face.

When he was just about drowned, he called on the birds for mercy and they flew away.[117]

. . . . . . . . . . . . . . . . . . . . . . . . . . . . . . . . . . . . . . . . . . . . . . . . . . . . . . . . . . . . . . . . . . . . . . . . . . . . . . . . . . . . . . . . . .

*There are variations to this story, but essentially it is the tale of the trickster insulting a rock and being chased by it. This is not always a stand-alone story among the Blackfoot, for in some accounts the narrative continues past the nighthawks' revenge, and tells of Napi meeting with the Sun spirit and killing buffalo by making them laugh to death.*

*As indicated in the Introduction, stories of the big rock can be found in varying forms among tribes all across North America, including the Stoney Nakoda, Assiniboine, Pawnee, Sioux, and Apache.*[118]

# The Sun's Leggings

After the trouble with the night birds, Napi started off again travelling eastward. There he came across a huge lodge, and when he went inside, an old man greeted him. Napi did not know it, but this was the Sun.

"What have you done to yourself?" asked the Sun. "You have no clothes on you."

"Well," answered Napi, "I was taking a good swim back at that big lake, and when I was in the water the prairie wolves ran away with my clothes. I saw your tepee here. That's why I came right over for you to help out with some clothes."

"All right," said the Sun. "I think I have some clothes to spare. Here's a robe for you and here is a shirt, leggings, and moccasins."

Napi noticed that the lodge was lined with all kinds of furs and holy objects, and among them was a beautiful pair of leggings. They were made of buffalo hide decorated with porcupine quills and red crow feathers. As soon as he saw them, Napi wanted them.

The Sun had no food in his lodge, so he invited Napi to hunt with him. He took down the wonderful leggings and said, "These are my hunting leggings. They are great medicine. All I have to do is to put them on and walk around a patch of brush, then the leggings set it on fire and drive the deer out so that I can shoot them." They went to a nearby brush, set it afire, and quickly the Sun had killed a white-tailed deer. Now Napi was even more anxious to have the leggings.

"Brother-in-law," he said, "give me those leggings."

"No, I will not give them to you."

"Yes, I must have them."

"No, these old leggings are of no use to you."

"Well, then," said Napi, "let me sleep here."

The Sun agreed, and Napi lay down to rest. In the middle of the night when all was in darkness he crept over and took the leggings, rolled them up, put them on his back, and slipped out of the lodge. He ran for much of the night, getting as far away from the Sun as possible. Finally he lay down to sleep again, using the leggings as his pillow.

"Old man, why are my leggings under your head?" enquired the Sun.

Napi looked around and was shocked to see that he was back in the Sun's lodge. "Oh," he replied, "I couldn't find anything for a pillow, so I just put these under my head."

The next evening, Napi tried again. He left the lodge and travelled all night, not settling down to sleep until just before daybreak. Four times he did this, and four times he awoke back in the Sun's lodge. He was a fool. He did not understand that the Sun's lodge is the whole world, and that he could never run beyond the Sun's sight.

After the fourth time, the Sun said, "Old Man, since you like my leggings so much, I will give them to you. Keep them." He warned Napi never to wear the leggings except to hunt. He added, "Whenever there is a famine I put them on. Then I look where there is a round bunch of trees, I run around it and then it burns. When it is all burned up, then there will lie some deer. Then I take the leggings off again. Then I put them away. At other times I never wear them." Napi was warned never to eat wild turnips and before wearing the leggings he had to use a certain type of grass to make incense.

Napi wasn't listening. All he could see were the wonderful leggings and he was anxious to try them on. He left the Sun's lodge and, hungry as usual, he pulled up some wild turnips and ate them. After walking a short distance he began to have trouble with gas, each fart being so strong that it blew him off his feet. He grabbed clumps of grass, but the farts threw him high in the air.

It finally passed, so he continued his journey until he came to a camp of people who were having a dance. He wanted to join them and show off his wonderful leggings, so he made a little fire to purify himself but used common grass for incense. He then donned his leggings, but as he danced among the people, a trail of fire followed him. He was frightened and called to the people to help him but they all ran away, crying that the "Old Man was trying to burn them up." Napi tried to escape, the flames burning his hair and clothes, until at last he jumped into Rock Lake. He tore off the leggings and they were destroyed.

"My leggings, those are the ones that burned," Napi explained to the people. "My brother-in-law gave them to me. He told me how to use them and I did not mind him. That's why they burned."[119]

......................................................................................................

*This is one of the few examples where Napi interacts with a recognized holy figure. Most accounts identify him as the Sun spirit and, indeed, if the tale is to make any sense, the Sun spirit is an essential figure. The fact that Napi could flee the stranger's lodge and yet wake up back in it next morning is a clear symbolism showing that Napi could never flee the Sun's lodge, or domain, which is the whole world.*

*There are a few Blackfoot accounts of this story, however, that do not identify the owner of the lodge, thus rendering the symbolism relatively meaningless. In de Jong he is identified as Napi's brother-in-law, but this may simply be another term for the Sun. Wissler and Duvall identify him simply as "the owner of the lodge" and "the stranger," while in White Bull he is an "old medicine man." In R.N. Wilson's account, the entire segment dealing with the Sun's lodge is missing and the story picks up at the point where Napi acquires the leggings.*

*The leggings themselves are variously described as being embroidered with "porcupine quills and pretty feathers," "of rough buffalo-hide with many crow-feathers on the sides," and "trimmed with red birds' feathers."*

*A similar version of this story exists among the Cheyenne, Stoney Nakoda, and Cree.*[120]

# The Buffalo Laugh

❁

After his adventure with the fire leggings, Napi, who was always hungry, decided to go hunting. He took his younger brother, Kit Fox, with him. They searched along the Red Deer River, and when they saw no game they moved over to the Little Bow River. For several days they killed nothing, and Napi was beginning to get desperate. It was autumn and he knew that winter was not far off.

They were walking along one day when Napi looked over a ridge and saw four big buffalo bulls lying down on the prairie grass. He dodged back out of sight and told Kit Fox what he had seen. He knew there was no way he could creep up on them, so he thought for a while, trying to find a way that he might trick them.

At last he said to Kit Fox, "My little brother, I can think of only one way to get these bulls. This is my plan, if you agree to it. I will pluck all the fur off you except one tuft on the end of your tail. Then you go over the hill and walk up and down in sight of these bulls, and you will seem so funny to them that they will laugh themselves to death."

Kit Fox wasn't very keen on the idea, but as he could not suggest anything better, he reluctantly agreed. Napi plucked him clean except for the ball at the end of his tail, then Kit Fox did as he was told, and paraded up and down on a ridge in front of the resting bulls. He pranced, played around, walked on his hind legs, and went through all kinds of antics. When the bulls saw him they were startled at first and stood up as if ready to flee. But curious, they stayed to watch, not knowing what to make of him. Then they began to laugh, a titter at first and then a roar of merriment. One by one they convulsed in laughter, then fell down exhausted, and died.

Napi came out of hiding and began to butcher the buffalo. "Ah, little brother," he said to Kit Fox, "you did splendidly. I don't wonder that the bulls laughed themselves to death. I nearly died myself as I watched you from the hill. You looked very funny."

As he spoke, Napi skinned the buffalo and cut the meat up to take back to camp. All the time he kept praising Kit Fox for his wonderful performance. Meanwhile, the weather was growing colder and a few snowflakes began swirling through the air. Kit Fox said nothing; his back was humped and his teeth were chattering with the cold. A wind sprang up from the north and the snow became heavier as the temperature continued to drop.

Napi continued to talk to his younger brother while he was working, but Kit Fox did not reply. He just stood there. Finally Napi stopped to stretch and said, "It's getting pretty cold. Well, we don't care. We have got all our winter's meat, and we will have nothing to do but feast and dance and sing until spring."

When Kit Fox did not reply, Napi became angry and shouted, "Why don't you answer me? Don't you hear me talking to you?"

When Kit Fox still said nothing, Napi stalked over to him, saying, "Can't you speak?" and roughly gave him a shove. Kit Fox fell over, his jaw jutting out and his teeth shining. He was frozen solid with the cold.

Napi said, "My younger brother has always been a laugher and that one was frozen with his face twisted."

...................................................................................................

*This is not one of the more popular Napi stories, although it was recorded by Uhlenbeck, Grinnell, and Wissler and Duvall.[121] It also appears among the Stoney Nakoda, where, like the Blackfoot version, the location is identified as the Little Bow River.[122]*

# The Man Who Wore Meat

---  ❀  ---

As Napi went along again, he met a rich young man going to war who was clothed entirely in buffalo meat. His shirt was belly fat, his leggings were back fat, his hat was a large piece of kidney, his moccasins were fine rump steaks, his belt was a large gut, and his fire bag was a tongue. Over all of this he wore a robe made of fat; his face was painted red with pemmican and white with grease. He had a bow made of a long buffalo rib and arrows of small guts that he carried in a quiver made of bull testicles.

Napi, who was always hungry, sidled up to the young man and begged for some meat.

"I am not going to give you my clothes," the man replied.

"Give me some of your arrows," Napi begged until finally the man relented and gave him one, which Napi immediately chewed up and swallowed.

"Give me some of your white paint," said Napi, and after he received it he begged for part of the man's leggings and some of his quiver. Bit by bit he got meat from the young man, then hurried behind a hill to make a fire and eat it.

When he was finished, Napi disguised himself and met the young man farther along the trail where he begged for some more pieces of his clothing. He did this three times, but when he tried the fourth time, he was unable to disguise his appearance and was refused. Not giving up, he tried another trick. Changing his tactics, he ran past the young man as fast as he could, shouting that they were being pursued. "We are almost overtaken by our enemies," he shouted. "We must save our lives. Just drop your quiver and arrows and throw all your clothes off, that you may run easily in order to save yourself."

The young man did as he was told and soon he was running naked across the prairie. Napi waited until he had gone out of sight, then went back, picked up all the meat, and had a feast.[123]

. . . . . . . . . . . . . . . . . . . . . . . . . . . . . . . . . . . . . . . . . . . . . . . . . . . . . . . . . . . . . . . . . . . . . . . . . . . . . . . .

*R.N. Wilson says that the rich young man going to war was a coyote. Uhlenbeck has a different version of the story. In his account, the young man's name is given as Fat (Pomis'). Napi accused him of having sexual relations with his wife, even though he had no wife. "No, I am not that person," argued Fat. In reply, Napi picked up a stick and threw it at the young man, threatening to kill him. Fat ran away, and as he fled, he shot at Napi with his arrows. When this didn't work, the young man threw away his hat, then his moccasins, leggings, and shirt. When he was naked, he hoped Napi would give up but he still pursued him. At last Fat jumped into a coulee, but when he struck the ground he exploded into grease. Napi ate the grease then returned along the trail to pick up the rest of the meat.*

# Napi and the Buffalo Jump

—— ❀ ——

As Napi went along again, he saw a man sitting on the edge of a cliff, singing and striking his rattles on the ground to lure the buffalo. As a herd came near, he sang, "Eeeee, let the buffalo fall down on each side of me." The herd split in two and passed on each side of him as they went over the cliff into a *piskun*, buffalo jump.

When Napi begged to learn the ritual, the man said, "It is not hard to do. I do this only when there is a famine coming, but not too often." He also warned Napi not to make a mistake and sing "Hit me between the ears," for this would cause the herd to run over him and kill him.

Napi took the rattles and wandered along until he came to a hill and a buffalo jump. He sat at the top of the hill, right on the edge of the cliff, where he beat the rattle and sang, "Eeeee, let the buffalo fall down on each side of me." Moments later, a herd of buffalo stampeded towards him, divided in two, and went over the cliff.

Pleased with his success, Napi went among the dead bodies and began to skin the fattest cows. He made a shade for himself, took a little of the meat, and began to cook it. When he had eaten, he left the rest of the meat behind and went wandering again. A short time later he came to another buffalo jump, so he decided to try his song again. He sat on the hill next to the jump and sang, "Eeeee, let the buffalo fall down on each side of me." Again the buffalo were lured by his singing and rattling and plunged over the cliff. After he had taken a few more choice pieces of meat, he travelled along until he came to a third buffalo jump and then a fourth, both with equally gratifying outcomes. In each instance the buffalo herd split in two, one half passing to his left and and the other half to his right.

Napi was having great fun. He remembered all the medicine man had told him, but ignored the warning to use this power infrequently and only when there was starvation. He also remembered the phrase that the medicine man told him not to use. Curious, he uttered the phrase, "Hit me between the ears," to see if anything would happen. Immediately a herd rushed to the edge, but instead of splitting in two the animals ran right over Napi and carried him to the bottom of the cliff. As he fell, he changed himself into a buffalo calf and lay on top of the other dead animals. The weather was bitterly cold, and soon Napi was frozen stiff.

After a while an old woman came along collecting firewood. She was surprised to see all the dead buffalo in the jump and thought the calf would make a nice robe for her grandson. She picked up the frozen carcass, and when she returned to her camp she said to her son-in-law, "Over there are buffalo that fell [off the bank] that you may skin them. Give part of them to the people camping here about."

Inside her lodge, the old woman hung the calf by its hind legs high up so that it would thaw out more quickly. Her grandson was delighted with the calf skin that soon would be his. He lay on his back, gazing up at the calf, but when he looked at its head, it spit down at him.

"Grandma," complained the little boy, "my skin here is spitting on me."

The grandmother told him, "No, my child, that is only the water leaking from it as it thaws."

The boy looked again, and the calf made a face at him.

"It is making faces down on me," said the boy.

"No, it is frozen that way, that is why it seems to make faces at you."

The boy looked again, and the calf stuck out its tongue.

"Grandma, the calf is putting its tongue out at me."

"No," replied his grandmother, "its tongue is frozen out of its mouth like that."

By this time, Napi was completely thawed, so he freed himself and jumped down, landing on the boy's stomach. It exploded like a gunshot, killing the boy as Napi ran from the lodge and made his escape.[124]

*Those who listen to this story have little sympathy for the little boy, who was obviously spoiled by his grandmother.*

*The first part of this story, dealing only with the use of the buffalo jump, is told by the Gros Ventre.*[125]

# Napi and the Bear

---

One day, as Napi was strolling along he came to a stream that was in flood. Confident that he could cope with the rushing water, he began to wade across but was only halfway over when he was caught by the strong current and swept off his feet. He cast aside his bow and other weapons in a desperate effort to reach the shore. When he finally succeeded, he lay on the bank, panting and mourning the loss of his bow, arrows, and knife.

He was hungry from all the exertion, so he set about to make some new weapons. He grabbed the first piece of wood he could find and fashioned a bow. With a handful of dried sticks he made arrows, and with a piece of flint he made a crude knife with a handle of driftwood. With these in hand, he started on his way.

Presently, he looked over a hill. Below him he saw a bear digging for roots. Deciding to have some fun, Napi cried out, "Oh, you dirty-assed bear!" then ducked out of sight. The bear looked around and, seeing no one, once again began to dig roots. Napi watched him for a few minutes, then called out again, "You dirty-assed bear!" The bear looked up quickly but not fast enough to see Napi as he ducked out of sight. Four times Napi played this trick on the bear, but on the fourth time the bear saw him and, snarling fiercely, started after him.

At first it was all a joke, but as the bear gained on him, Napi became worried. Placing an arrow into his crudely made bow he tried to shoot, but the rotten bow broke in two and the arrow sailed crazily away. As the bear came closer, Napi tried to stab it with his knife, but the weapon fell to pieces in his hands. Now running for his life, Napi called to the animals to help him, but they remembered the nasty tricks he had played on them, so no one came to his rescue. Finally, Napi came to a huge rock and, hoping to escape, he ran around it. But the bear was right behind him and soon they were running round and round the rock until they wore a deep rut in the ground.

Almost out of breath, Napi saw a buffalo bull's horn lying on the ground. Swiftly he picked it up, put it on his head, then turned around and bellowed loudly. The bear was so surprised and frightened that it immediately defecated. "That is what you bears will do when you are scared," said Napi, and to the rock he said, "This is the way you rocks shall always be after this, with a big hole all around you."[126]

......................................................................................................................

*Some skeptics would say the depressions around the rock were actually made by buffalo that came to the rock to rub against its sides. This is how Grinnell explains them:*

> *Around these great boulders the buffalo used to walk from time to time, rubbing against the rough surface of the rock to scratch themselves, as a cow rubs itself against a post or as a horse rolls on the ground—for the pleasant feeling that the rubbing of the skin gives it. As the buffalo walked around these boulders their hoofs loosened the soil, and this loosened soil—the dust—was blown away by the constant winds of summer. So, around most of these boulders, much of the soil is gone, leaving a deep trench, at the bottom of which are stones and gravel, too large to be moved by the wind.[127]*

# Napi and the Bullberries

---

Napi was thirsty after all the excitement, so he went to a stream for a drink. As he leaned over, he saw large bunches of ripe bullberries hanging from their branches under the water. He said to himself, "I will dive in and get those bullberries." He took off his moccasins and clothing and dived to the bottom but, feeling around, he could not find them. Back on shore he looked down and saw that the bullberries were still there, invitingly delicious. "Those bullberries must be very deep down," he said. The second time, Napi dived even deeper and groped around the streambed but, as before, no berries. This made him angry and determined.

To make sure he could stay under the water for a long time he tied big stones to his legs and neck. When he jumped in he sank right to the bottom, grinning in anticipation as he thought of the elusive berries. But as he searched and searched he found nothing, only water. When his breath was exhausted, Napi decided to return to the surface but the rocks held him down. Suddenly he knew he was in trouble. Frantically, he tore at the ropes, and he was almost drowned before he managed to break free. Full of water, he bobbed to the surface and pulled himself to shore, where he lay on his back, panting in exhaustion.

As he lay there, Napi looked up and saw the bullberries right above his head. That is when he realized that all this time he had been fooled by the reflection of the berries in the water. "These are the ones because of whom I was almost drowned," he said. "I shall thoroughly punish

you." He cut a long stick and angrily began to beat the bush, punishing it for having tricked him. "After this," he said, "the people shall beat you in this way when they want to gather berries."[128]

. . . . . . . . . . . . . . . . . . . . . . . . . . . . . . . . . . . . . . . . . . . . . . . . . . . . . . . . . . . . . . . . . . . . . . . . . . . . . . . . . . . . . . . . . . . . . . . . .

*Grinnell explains more about how the berries were gathered: "The Blackfeet women, when gathering bullberries, spread robes under the bushes and beat the branches with sticks, knocking off the berries, which fall on the robes."*

*This story is told by several North American tribes—the Arapaho, Gros Ventre, Assiniboine, Apache, Ojibwa, and Cheyenne—and, indeed, in other parts of the world. According to the Cheyenne, the fruit was plums not bullberries.*[129]

# The Big Arrow

───────────── ❁ ─────────────

Napi continued on until he came to a chickadee sitting with an elk antler. When he asked the bird what he was doing with the antler, the chickadee answered, "It is my bow." There was a large lodgepole pine tree lying beside the antler, and when Napi asked the bird what he was going to do with it, the chickadee answered, "It is my arrow."

Napi laughed at the idea of such a tiny bird having a huge bow and arrow, but the chickadee argued, "I may be a little bird but I am a strong one, for the [eagle] is my inferior."

Napi said, "Oh, you little conceited fellow to call the greatest of all birds your inferior. You cannot lift your arrow nor bend your bow. I would like to see you shoot with them." He added, "Why don't you try to shoot me?"

The chickadee told Napi to walk a few paces away so he could aim and shoot the arrow at him.

"Here?" asked an amused Napi, after walking a short distance.

"Further away."

"Here?"

"Further away."

"Here?" said Napi, growing impatient.

He reached a nearby ridge, but the chickadee still wasn't satisfied and told him to go to the next ridge, and then to the next. When he reached the fourth ridge, Napi forgot why he was walking and forgot about the little bird with the big bow and arrow. He continued to walk along the trail and after a while he heard a noise behind him. Looking back, he was surprised to see the big arrow coming straight for him, guided by the little chickadee who was riding on top. Napi ran as fast as he could but the arrow followed after him as he swung to the left and the right. At last he saw a coyote den and dived in just as the arrow struck him in the backside and pushed him out the other side.

When he emerged, Napi changed his appearance and went crying to the chickadee, who was busy trying to pull the arrow out of the coyote den. When the bird asked him why he was crying, Napi said he was unhappy because the chickadee had a big arrow and he didn't have any. So the bird gave him the arrow, but warned, "You must only use it when you are hungry and you can only shoot it four times, and each shot must be a long time after the last shot."

As usual, Napi ignored the words of warning and happily took the arrow to a herd of buffalo he had seen nearby. He shot the arrow and succeeded in killing a bull. He ate only the succulent parts, then went out to shoot a second bull, then a third, and finally a fourth. On his fifth try the arrow became so heavy he could not lift it, let alone shoot it. But he was not completely crestfallen, for as he dragged the arrow away he said, "At least I have plenty of firewood."[130]

..................................................................................................

*In de Jong's version, two boys owned the elk antler bow and pine tree arrow that they gave to Napi. He tried to use the bow and arrow four times, and on the fourth time he could not lift either of them. Angrily, he chopped at the arrow and said, "Henceforth you shall be treated like this by the women who are to cut down their lodge-poles." To the elk antler he said about all antlers, "You shall be cut to pieces by the women who will use them as scraper-handles."*

*This tale is also told by the Cheyenne and Apache. For the Gros Ventre, this legend is interwoven with the story of the big rock, and they also combine this tale with the one about the nighthawks stopping the big rock.[131]*

# Napi Loses His Eyes

---  ✿  ---

Napi was taking a long walk in a forest when he heard the loud singing of a bird. Following the sound, he saw a chickadee sitting on the bottom branch of a dry tree. The little bird sang, "*Ni-po-makee*" ("chickadee"), and its eyes flew out of its head and onto a branch of the old tree. The little bird then sang, "Shot off my both eyes, / Away high upon this dry tree."

He paused for a moment, then sang out, "*Mutsuki-pi-po-makee*" ("chickadee, come back") and the eyes flew back into their sockets, after which he sang, "My eyes come off, / And back to their place again."

Napi stood for a while, impressed by the unusual actions of the little bird. At last he said to himself, "I'm going to walk towards him crying for mercy. I know he will have pity on me." So, with tears running down his face, Napi walked towards the chickadee, crying that the bird was his little brother.

"Yes," said the chickadee, "I know we are brothers. What do you want from me?"

"Little brother," he begged, "teach me how to do that."

"Well, Old Man," replied the bird, "it is not hard to do."

The chickadee taught Napi the words that would make the eyes fly into a tree and the words that would bring them back. He told Napi to repeat the words over and over so that he would not forget them. "Oh, that's easy to learn," he said. "I have learned them already."

When they were finished, the chickadee warned Napi, "You are only allowed to do this four times." But the trickster paid no attention; he was too anxious to try out this newfound power. When he came to a tall, straight tree he called out, "*Ni-po-makee*," and his eyes jumped out of his head and into the tree. He sang the chickadee's song, then said, "*Mutsuki-pi-po-makee*," and his eyes popped back into their sockets.

Napi was delighted and couldn't wait to try it again. When he came to another tree he called out, "*Ni-po-makee*," and again his eyes jumped out of his head and into the tree. The chickadee's song and the phrase *Mutsuki-pi-po-makee* brought him back to normal.

It was a fun game and Napi enjoyed it thoroughly. He tried it a third time and then a fourth time, both with the desired results. Recalling the chickadee's caution, Napi thought, "Why did that bird tell me to do this only four times? He has no sense. I will do it again."

So, heedless of the little bird's warning, Napi sent his eyes into a tree for the fifth time. After a few moments he called out, "*Mutsuki-pi-po-makee*," but nothing happened; the eyes did not come back. "*Mutsuki-pi-po-makee*," he shouted again, his voice echoing through the forest. Nothing. For hours he yelled until his throat was sore, until at last he gave up. He was stone blind.

Napi stumbled through the forest, crying and bewailing his fate. Covering his eye sockets with a bandage, he stood alone, making signs in the hope that someone would help him. At last a woman saw him and said to herself, "He is making signs to me to come." She walked right up to him but was surprised when he kept signalling.

"What's wrong with you?" she asked. "I'm right here with you."

"Oh, I saw you coming," he lied, "but I saw another woman way up this side of that big ridge. Just to keep me company, that's why I'm waving at her."[132]

The woman noticed Napi's bandage for the first time. "I want you to lead me back to the camps," Napi said. "I nearly went blind, but I can see a little now. I was fighting a prairie fire the other day. The smoke got into my eyes and hurt them very bad."

The woman took pity on him and said, "All right, my brother, I'll take good care of you."

They were a long way from the camps, so Napi suggested they make a shelter for the night. He complained he was hungry and asked the woman to make a bow and arrows so he could kill a buffalo. When they were ready Napi had the woman aim it for him and he killed a fat young cow. But by this time the woman was suspicious of Napi, so she lied and said, "You missed her." She then directed him to another buffalo, a poor skinny cow, and he killed that one as well.

Now she had enough skins to make a temporary lodge, so she commenced butchering the two animals. Meanwhile, she told Napi to go and fetch some lodgepoles and make a frame for a lodge. Napi did as he was told, collected some poles, and started to put up a shelter. When he ran out of poles he went for more, but when he came back he couldn't find the original shelter. After groping around for a while, he finally gave up and started to build a new shelter. On his next trip out, the same thing happened, and soon there were lodge frames scattered all over the place.

When the woman came back from her butchering, she asked Napi if he was expecting a bunch of visitors.

"No," replied Napi. "You women are so hard to please that I made a number so that you could take your choice."

While the woman was butchering, she had set aside the kidneys from the fat cow for herself but gave Napi the ones from the skinny cow. Each sat around the fire cooking their kidneys, when Napi noticed that hers smelled better than his. Quietly, he sharpened a stick then thrust it into her kidney and took it away from her. He then proceeded to eat both kidneys.

He told the woman to boil the buffalo hoofs, and once they were cleaned he painted them red and made them into a necklace. He told her to wear it on the back of her dress at all times. He said this was powerful medicine that would prevent her from becoming pregnant. He said this because he wanted her to wear something that made noise so he could hear where she was.

During the afternoon Napi and the woman rested in the lodge. Napi laid his head on her lap and asked her to pick the lice out of his hair. She obliged, and it felt so nice that Napi soon fell asleep. As he lay there, the woman became curious about his eyes, wondering if they were healing. Carefully, she raised his bandage and instead of eyes, all she saw were empty sockets.

"All this time he has been lying to me," she said in shock. "He told me he only had sore eyes. He's stone blind."

Terrified, she slipped out from under his head and made for the door. Napi awoke, and realizing what had happened, ran after her. The rattles on her dress let him know where she was going, and no matter how many times she changed course, he was always behind her. At last, she realized that the rattles were giving her away, so she pulled them off and threw them over an embankment and into a deep river. Napi followed the sound and plunged head first into the water, while the woman safely made her escape.

Napi had a hard time getting out of the water and almost drowned. He drifted downstream for a distance and finally came to shore beside a round hill. Sitting there was a coyote who had a sore paw. Deciding to have a little fun, the coyote tripped the blind Napi as he walked along, and when he fell down, the coyote pushed its infected paw into his nose.

"Guess I know this place by the smell," said Napi. "It is near my brother-in-law's buffalo jump; there is always a carcass or two lying stinking around near it."

Napi walked towards the smell but the coyote kept tripping him. After this had happened two or three times, Napi was sure he was being tricked. "I'll fix him," he said to himself, and pretended to follow the smell. The next time the coyote tripped him Napi made a quick grab and caught the animal by the head. He took one of the coyote's eyes and was elated that once again he could see.

Now he was hungry again, so he decided to go to a nearby village and beg for some meat. However, when the people saw him with an empty socket for an eye, they were frightened and ran away. "I will not hurt you; come back!" he cried, but it did no good. Angrily, Napi stomped back to the coyote and said, "Here, you are to blame for this. You only gave me one eye, and scared the people away." With that outburst, he grabbed the other eye and left the coyote blind.[133]

. . . . . . . . . . . . . . . . . . . . . . . . . . . . . . . . . . . . . . . . . . . . . . . . . . . . . . . . . . . . . . . . . . . . . . . . . . . . . . . . .

*This is one of the most popular and enduring Napi stories. In R.N. Wilson's version, Napi's eyes flew into a willow bush where they turned white and became pussywillows. This, said Wilson, was the origin of the pussywillow. Wissler and Duvall said the coyote willingly loaned one of its eyes to Napi so that he could hunt, but when Napi went to the camps, he frightened everyone away. He returned to the coyote and blamed him, then took the coyote's other eye and left it blind. Cecil Black Plume offered a unique ending to the story. He said that after Napi's eyes flew into the tree, the magpies found them and ate them. Uhlenbeck provided a happier ending to the story. He said that when Napi got the coyote's eyes, he went back to the tree and recovered his own. He then returned to the coyote and gave it its eyes back.*

*In the story according to the Gros Ventre, an unidentified bird showed the trickster how to throw his eyes into a tree. A mouse came to his rescue and donated its eyes, and after the trickster found his own eyes, he returned the borrowed ones to the mouse. The Cheyenne say the trickster learned from a medicine man how to throw his eyes. After performing the trick four times, he came to a village, and to show his newfound powers, he threw his eyes away for a fifth time. They went into a tree, where a crow promptly ate them. He got an eye from a mouse, but it was so small he could only see a tiny ray of light. Then he got an eye from a buffalo, but it was too big for his socket, and the two different eyes gave him a headache. He then went home to his wife who told him to stop fooling around and trying to impress people with his tricks.*

*The Assiniboine say that four boys gave the trickster the power to throw his eyes into the trees. When he abused this power and the eyes would not return, one of the boys took pity on him and used one of his own eyes to rescue the trickster's eyes. The boy then took away the trickster's power to ever do the trick again. In an Apache version of the story, rabbits were the ones throwing their eyes into the trees, not a bird.*[134]

# Napi, the Kit Fox, and the Old Women

After recovering his eyes, Napi began walking until he met a kit fox who had some curious ornaments made from hollow sticks and bark hung all over his head, ears, and nose, and around his neck. Napi asked the kit fox why he was wearing such curious objects and he explained that these were his power. To procure meat, all he had to do was to find a buffalo and the ornaments would work like a charm.

Napi doubted this, but he was hungry, so he begged the kit fox to let him take the objects so he could get meat. The kit fox agreed, but warned Napi that he should use this power only four times and not more than twice in a day. He should also use it only when he was extremely hungry. Napi was always hungry, so he paid no attention to the warnings. He put on the ornaments, and as he approached a small herd of buffalo he started to shake his head. A bull took one look at Napi and began to laugh. The sight was so ridiculous that he could not help himself. Every time Napi shook his head the bull laughed louder and louder, until finally he laughed himself to death.

Pleased with his success, Napi took only a small portion of the meat, then looked for another bull. Like the first, he laughed until he died. The same thing happened with two more bulls. Then, ignoring the caution given to him by the kit fox, he tried a fifth time, Napi approached another bull and shook his head, but this time the bull did not laugh; instead he was infuriated by Napi's actions and roared in anger. As the buffalo tried to gore him, Napi dodged out of the way and ran for his life with the buffalo in hot pursuit. When he finally escaped, Napi took off the ornaments and threw them away.

He continued on for only a short distance when he came in sight of two women picking berries. There was not enough time for them to hide or run away, so the women decided to play dead. When Napi looked down at them lying on the ground he said, "Poor women. These are nice women. It is too bad they are dead." When he touched them he found they were warm and commented, "Oh, they have just died!"

He turned them over several times but he could see no wounds. He then removed their dresses and looked over their bodies from their chins down to their legs. His eyes finally rested on their vaginas. "Oh," he said, "no wonder they died. Here are the wounds." He stuck his finger into one of the vaginas and said, "Oh, I see what is wrong now. Someone stabbed her right here with a flint knife. It's getting a little odoriferous."

"I pity these poor women," he continued. "They were too young to die. I must try to doctor them back to life again." He decided to carry them to the river to try revive to them with water. He thought that if he could save them, he would have two wives.

He picked up one of the women and began carrying her on his back. One of her arms hung loosely over his shoulder, and as he walked it swung freely. Taking advantage of the situation, the woman swung her arm so that it pounded Napi's nose every time he moved until it started to bleed. Not knowing the woman was still alive, he thought her limp arm was just swinging on its own.

Finally reaching the river, Napi laid her on the ground and went back for the other one. No sooner was he out of sight than the woman jumped up and made her escape. When Napi got back to the place where the second woman had been lying, he found that she too had run away.

"Ah, you women," shouted Napi, "come back and lay down as you were before." But they didn't.[135]

# Flying with the Geese

As Napi travelled along, he came to a large lake where many geese and other birds were gathering into flocks. When he asked them what they were doing, Goose Chief explained they were flying south for the winter. Napi begged to join them and the chief agreed if he would wear feathers, just as they did. Napi was happy to oblige, so each goose gave him a feather until he was completely covered.

Before setting out, Goose Chief warned Napi, "When we fly over the Indian camps, you must not look down, no matter how much you may want to see what is going on."

At last they were ready to leave. Flocks of geese rose gracefully into the air, forming familiar V-patterns in the sky as they headed south. Napi was among them, joyfully soaring through the air and relishing the thought of spending the winter in a warm climate. When they passed over an Indian village, Napi remembered what the chief had told him and looked straight ahead; never once did he glance down.

When they came to a second village, the people were amazed to see Napi flying among the geese and shouted and waved to him as he passed by. Napi heard them and, proud of the way he was flying through the skies, he looked down to see the people who were waving at him. In that instant he lost his balance and his feathers scattered as he plunged to earth. His trip was suddenly over.[136]

*One Blackfoot version states that the birds were cranes.*

*The Stoney Nakoda tell a longer version of the story. In it, the geese were gathering together in preparation for their migration south when Inktomi, the trickster, found them. He went to their chief and begged to be taken along, so a council was called to discuss the matter. One goose said he was too fat to fly, another that he was too heavy, another that he had no wings, and others said the trip was too long and too far. Finally the chief decided that Inktomi could accompany them but he had to make his own wings.*

*With the advice of a goose elder, Inktomi gathered goose feathers and made a pair of wings. He then joined the young geese who were swimming in a lake, and from them he learned how to fly. Four times he flew around the lake and learned to honk like a goose.*

*When they were ready to leave, the chief told Inktomi to take his place to his left and to never look down and never act proud. Four days after they started their flight, the geese flew over a Stoney Nakoda camp and the people were amazed at the size of the Inktomi-goose and praised him. Inktomi heard their words and was very proud. He looked down at the people and suddenly he fell to the ground and was killed. For three days the Stoney Nakoda threw ashes on Inktomi's body and mocked him, but on the fourth day an old woman washed his wounds and brought him back to life.[137]*

*An Assiniboine story tells of Inktomi asking to fly with the geese and being told, "Flying is difficult." Eight geese finally carried him aloft but knowing of the tricks he played, they dumped him into a mud hole.[138]*

*A second Assiniboine version combines stories that are told as separate accounts by the Blackfoot. In this version, the trickster begged the geese to let him fly with them. As they went over a village, people started shooting at them, and the geese dropped the trickster into a mud hole. Only his anus was visible, but everyone recognized him. When mice tried to climb into his anus he shook them off and sat down beside a rock. When the rock asked him for a gift, he refused, so it kept him prisoner for four days. Inktomi asked some birds flying over to help him and promised to give them his daughter. So the birds flapped their wings and caused a wind to blow that shattered the rock to pieces. Inktomi then told the birds, "I have no daughter," and walked away.[139]*

# The Red-Eyed Duck

❀

Napi walked along the bank of a river with a large pack on his back. When he came to a place where the river widened, he saw many ducks swimming about, but he paid no attention to them. But the ducks were curious.

"Who is that going along there with a pack on his back?" a duck asked.

"That must be Old Man," said another.

A duck called out to him and asked him where he was going.

"I am going on farther," he said. "I have been sent for."

"What have you got in your pack?"

"Those are my songs. Some people have asked me to come and sing for them."

"Stop for a while and sing for us," begged the duck, "and we can have a dance." The duck kept pleading for Napi to stop but he insisted he had to leave.

"I am in a hurry," he said. "I cannot stop now."

After the fourth request from the duck, Napi agreed. "I will stop for a little while and sing for you, and you can dance."

All the ducks came ashore and stood in a circle while Napi sang. After he had finished the third song, he told the ducks, "Now, this next song is a medicine song, and while you dance you must keep your eyes shut. No one must look. If anyone opens his eyes and looks, his eyes will turn red."

The ducks did as they were told. As Napi sang, the ducks danced in a circle with their eyes closed. As he was singing, Napi picked up a stick and as each duck passed him, he clubbed it on the head and threw its body into the circle.

One of the littlest ducks could sense a commotion near him, so it opened its eyes just as Napi was throwing another duck onto the pile.

"Run! Run!" shouted the little duck. "Old Man is killing us!" Immediately all the other ducks flew away, but not before Napi had grabbed the little duck that had disobeyed his orders. As punishment he turned its eyes red, and from that time on a new variety of duck had been created: the horned grebe.

Napi gathered all the ducks he had killed and found a nice place to camp. He built a fire. Afterward, he brushed aside the coals and buried a few of the ducks in the ashes, setting aside the others for later. Then, satisfied, he lay down to take a nap until the ducks were cooked.

As he slept, a coyote came prowling by and saw the pile of uncooked ducks. Quietly, it ate them one by one until they were gone. Then, smelling meat cooking, it found the rest of the ducks in the ashes. It dug up each one, ate the meat inside the skin, then filled it with sand and reburied it. When he was finished, he went away.

Napi awoke, hungrily anticipating a feast of ducks but when he saw the coyote tracks around the fire, he knew that his pile of uncooked ducks would be gone.

"I was lucky," Napi said to himself, "that I put some of those to roast under the fire." He dug them up, but when he took his first bite, all he got was a mouthful of sand.

So Napi went hungry again.[140]

..........................................................................................................

*In the Menomoni story, Nanabozho was busy killing the birds when a helldiver opened its eyes and screamed a warning. As punishment, its eyes turned red and its tail was cut short. In a Cree account, the little bird is identified as a waterhen, and among the northern Saulteaux it was a loon. A similar story is told by the Gros Ventre, except that those dancing included ducks, prairie chickens, and rabbits, with a prairie chicken giving the warning. This version ends with the trickster punishing his anus with a burning stick, which, among the Blackfoot, is part of another story of Napi.[141]*

# Napi and the Geese

⁂

Napi went along again until he came to a lake where a large flock of geese were swimming. He was still hungry and thought to himself, "How shall I get these geese?"

He began to cry until the leader of the geese sent someone to find out what was troubling him. "What happened?" asked the messenger. "Why are you crying?"

Napi told him that the Goose Chief had been killed in battle and he was mourning for him. He said he had come to the lake to enlist the help of other geese in going to war to avenge the death of their leader. When the geese heard the news, they agreed to go to war with Napi. Before they left, Napi told them to sit in a row to smoke a peace pipe. Once that was done they marched for a long distance until they were far out of sight of the lake, at which time Napi told them to stop. They were instructed to sit in a row while they smoked the peace pipe once more.

This time, Napi said that some of them were very tired and did not have the strength to go to war. "I will examine you now," he told them. "I will look through your feathers to recognize which ones are fat and which ones are lean, so the lean ones can go back home because they are not ready for war, but the fat ones will go to war with me because they are strong."

Napi walked along the row of geese and felt the breasts of each one. The fat ones he told to stay and the thin ones he sent home. Then, with the fat ones around him, he told them to close their eyes and perform a war dance that he had taught them. As they danced, Napi walked behind each one and killed them with a club.

Afterwards he made a fire, plucked the feathers, and ate his fill.[142]

...........................................................................................................

*In de Jong, the birds were both geese and ducks, while R.N. Wilson says the person killed in battle was Napi's son, not the goose chief. Otherwise, the stories are quite consistent. An Assiniboine story is similar except that it continues with the story of the lame fox outwitting the trickster in a race. For the Blackfoot, this is part of the story associated with Napi killing the gophers.*

# The Chief's Daughter

---
⚘
---

As Napi walked along, he came to a buffalo jump where the people had just made a kill. Men were butchering and women were cutting meat and placing it on racks to dry. Still others were preparing to tan some of the hides. Napi went into the lodge of three old women. All were widows, their husbands having died or been killed in war. They were very poor, but today they had been given some meat from an old buffalo bull. The women placed this before Napi together with a piece of belly fat.

"*Hai'-yah ho!*" he cried. "You treat me badly. A whole *pis'kun* of fat buffalo just killed; the camp red with meat, and here these old women give me tough bull meat and belly fat to eat. Hurry now! Roast me some ribs and a piece of back fat."

The women explained that all they had were pieces of meat from poor cows or old bulls that the others in camp had left for them. "Ah! How poor! You are very poor," sympathized Napi. "Take courage now. I will help you. Tomorrow they will run another band into the *pis'kun*. I will be there. I will kill the fattest cow, and you can have it all."

The old women were happy and looked forward to the hunt the next day. "We will have marrow guts and liver," they said excitedly. "We will have paunch and fat kidneys."

The next morning, another herd was stampeded over the cliff and everyone set to work to butcher the new kills. But where was Napi? In spite of his promise to the old women, he was nowhere to be seen at the buffalo jump. Instead, he was prowling around the camp, which was almost deserted. The only people left behind were some old women and the chief's daughter, who was sleeping in her father's lodge. A spoiled child, she was lying on a robe of pure white buffalo skin with a pillow made of a beautiful beaver pelt filled with buffalo hair. All her clothes were the finest in the camp.

Napi crept into the girl's lodge carrying a stick that he had covered with excrement and rubbed it on the white robe. The smell awakened the girl and seeing it, she begged Napi, "Old Man, pity me. Old Man, wipe it off."

"It is too dirty for me," he replied. "I shall not wipe it off." But then he reconsidered and said to her, "Pay me first, then I shall wipe it off."

"I will give you this fine beaded shirt of my father's," she said, but Napi refused.

She pleaded with him, offering her father's best horse, her beaver pelt pillow, her moccasins, her leggings, and even her fancy dress if he would remove the excrement from her robe, but he refused them all.

"See all my father's weapons hanging there," she said, "his shield, war headdress, scalps, and knife." No, said Napi, he did not want them.

Finally, in desperation, the girl offered to give Napi her father's youngest wife, her near mother, and her own mother, but again Napi refused. Then she offered herself, and Napi immediately accepted her offer and cleaned the robe.

As Napi lay beside her on the robe, the girl was frightened by the length of his penis. "Old Man," she said, "do not put in the whole of it. Tie a string across to shorten it for me." Obligingly, Napi did as she asked, but during sexual intercourse he untied the string and tore her to death. Satisfied, he wrapped a bandage around his head and went to see the old women, complaining of feeling ill. They put him to bed and added fuel to the fire to keep him warm.

A short time later the people returned from the buffalo jump, and when the chief entered his lodge, he found his daughter dead and covered in blood. Seeing the nature of her wound, he knew that only Napi could have inflicted such damage. Aware that the trickster could change his appearance, the chief decided that his penis would be his downfall.

"Now to-day," he announced, " we will find out who killed this child. Every man in this camp—every young man, every old man—must come and jump across the creek; and if any one does not jump across, if he falls in the water, that man is the one who did the killing." He knew that Napi, with his large penis, could never make the jump.

The men formed a line ready to jump over the creek. The whole village was there, waiting to see the perpetrator of the foul deed fall into the water and be killed. Then someone noticed that Napi was not in the line. Two young men went to the lodge of the three old women and found him lying on a bed.

"Old Man," they said, "a child has been killed. We have all got to jump to find out who did it. The chief has sent for you. You will have to jump, too."

"*Ki-yo*," said one of the old women, "Old Man is very sick. Go off, and let him alone. He is so sick he could not kill meat for us to-day."

"Yes," argued another. "See how he shivers and hear how he groans."

Meanwhile, Napi put on a good act and it seemed as though he was at death's door.

"It can't be helped," the young men replied. "The chief says every one must jump."

As Napi reluctantly made his way to the creek, he was very frightened and wasn't sure what to do next. Then he met a tiny chickadee who also was going to the creek and he got an idea. He praised the little bird and asked for some of its power. In exchange he said how much better the bird would look and how everyone would admire him if he had Napi's penis. The chickadee was flattered and agreed to exchange his tiny penis for Napi's big one.

When they reached the creek, the whole camp watched how one after another successfully made the jump. When it came to Napi's turn, he made an easy leap, much to the consternation of the chief who believed he was guilty. Then came the chickadee. Weighted down by Napi's penis, he jumped less than halfway across the creek before falling into the water. He was at once seized as the guilty party but loudly protested his innocence.

"Wait! Hold on!" screamed the little bird, as the warriors prepared to kill him. "Let me speak a few words. Every one knows I am a good jumper. I can jump farther than any one; but Old Man asked me for some of my power, and I gave it to him, and he gave me [his penis]. That is why I fell into the creek."

The warriors immediately grabbed Napi and were about to put him to death when he cried, "Wait, what will you gain by killing me? Set me free and I will doctor the girl and she will come alive again as well as ever."

Napi went into the chief's lodge and was followed by the warriors, who did not trust him. To prevent his escape, the chief placed two old men armed with spears at the of back the lodge, where they stood facing each other. At the doorway were two old women armed with clubs, also facing each other. Napi built a large fire and hung a large piece of belly fat close by so that the hot grease would drip into two big bowls. Meanwhile, the warriors were told to strip naked and stand facing away from the centre of the lodge.

When all was in readiness Napi began to sing, "*Ahk-sa'-kē-wah, Ahk-sa'-kē-wah, Ahk-sa'-kē-wah*—I don't care, I don't care, I don't care." The old men did as Napi told them and kept time with their spears, moving them up and down, while the old women also did what they were told, pretending to hit each other with their clubs. This went on for some time, and all the while the belly fat was being rendered into grease.

"Now I want every one to shut their eyes," said Napi. "No one can look. I am going to begin the real doctoring."

He took the two bowls and splashed the hot grease on the backs of the warriors. While they howled in pain, the two warriors thrust their spears at Napi but succeeded only in stabbing each other. Napi grabbed a buffalo robe and threw it through the door. The two old women, thinking it was Napi, swung their clubs but succeeded only in killing each other.

In the confusion, Napi ran away but was pursued by others in the camp. Soon he came to a place where some women were dressing hides.

They caught him, but when he promised to give each of them thirty elk teeth, they let him go. Farther along some boys playing an arrow and hoop game stopped him, but he told them he was in a foot race with the people who were chasing him. He said if they let him go, he would win the race and he would reward them all with arrows, feathers, and eagle quills. They freed him, and so Napi escaped.[143]

........................................................................................

*Neither Grinnell nor Wilson make any reference to the chief's daughter being raped, merely that she was killed. Grinnell states that the chickadee received something from Napi, not his penis but a necklace, while Wissler and Duvall say the object was Napi's lariat (another word for Napi's penis).*

*Some interesting questions arise from this story. The apparent participants are people, presumably humans, so why does a chickadee take part with all the appearance of being equal to others in the camp? Is it possible that these were all animals and the girl was a female beaver, such as occurs in another Napi story? In the retelling of this story, have the animals taken on a human form? More than likely, this story came from another tribe where Coyote was the trickster and all the participants were animals; it was adapted to Napi but did not quite fit.*

# Wolves on the Ice

— ✿ —

As Napi went along, he came to a river that was partly frozen over. On the ice were a number of wolves who were playing a game. They would run quickly, spin around, and pick up something that oozed from a crack in the ice. They swallowed it and continued on with the game.

"What are they doing?" Napi asked himself. Keeping out of sight, he ran towards the river to get a closer look. Then he saw, to his surprise, that the wolves were picking up pieces of fresh tallow and eating it.

"Oh, oh, let me do the same," he cried.

"Come on, Old Man," replied a wolf. "It is not hard to do. Now we shall give you this dance of ours. This river here is the only one on which you should do it. Do not do it on any other river." He was told to perform the dance in the morning when the ice is smooth but not to do it too often, only when there was a famine.

Napi went onto the ice and danced as the wolves had taught him. He sang, "Ice must crack, ice must crack, *hù-wi'*, *hù-wi'*." Then, as the pieces of tallow oozed through the cracks in the ice, Napi spun around, scooped up the pieces, and swallowed them. When the wolves had gone, Napi did this dance three more times, each time scooping up a mouthful of tallow. Then, ignoring the warning of the wolves, he decided to try another river to get more tallow. He danced and spun, danced and spun, but no cracks appeared in the ice and nothing happened, so he went back to the first river to try again.

There he was met by the wolves, who said, "Old Man, you did not mind what we told you. And so we take our dance back from you. Now this river will not remain here any longer. We shall go away with it, up to the sky we shall go with it. The people who are now growing up will see it. It will be called the Wolf-Road."

As soon as they said this, the wolves and the river disappeared. That night, when he looked into the sky, Napi saw that the Wolf-Road had been laid out in the middle of the sky. This became known as the Milky Way but was always called the Wolf-Road by the Blackfoot people.[144]

*Only de Jong ends the story with the origin of the Milky Way. In all the other tales, Napi danced once too often, the ice broke, and he almost drowned. This ending of the story is more in keeping with the tone of other Napi stories. The Wolf-Road figures in serious cultural stories, such as Tail Feathers Woman returning from the sky with the ritual of the Sun Dance. According to McClintock, she came via the Wolf-Road. It is unlikely that Napi would ever be associated with anything as religious as this.*

# The Sleeping Beaver

---

Napi continued on. He came to a river, and on the other side, he saw a female beaver sleeping. Calling a muskrat to his side, he said, "My younger brother, take my penis here and swim across to that place over there where that beaver is sleeping. Then put my penis to her vulva. When you are putting it into her vulva, bite it. And then I shall push."

Napi could extend his penis to any length, so he handed the head to the muskrat and he began to swim across the river. However, the current was swift and carried him downstream. This made Napi angry and he scolded his little brother-in-law, the muskrat, who did not appreciate it. After all, he was only trying to help.

He decided to teach Napi a lesson, so instead of placing the head of Napi's penis at the entrance to the sleeping beaver's vulva, he took it instead to a nearby thicket of thorns. Then, as instructed, he bit the end of the penis and Napi thrust it forward with all his might. As he howled in pain, the muskrat said, "That is what you get for fooling with relations."[145]

........................................................

*About this story, Wissler and Duvall comment that Napi had "ploughed out a deep trail." Wilson, reflecting Victorian sensitivities, says that the muskrat carried Napi's foot across the river for the purpose of kicking the beaver to death. In the Assiniboine version, a bird was sent to insert the penis into the beaver but it woke up and swam away. In a Cree version, the female character is a freshwater clam.*

# Girls Picking Strawberries

---

One day, as Napi was walking along, he saw some girls in the distance picking strawberries. He crept up close to them and extended his penis underground until it came up in the middle of a strawberry patch and became stained with strawberry juice.

One of the girls noticed the head of the penis and exclaimed, "Oh, here is a big one."[146]

As they crowded around it, another girl said, "Let us bite it." And they bit it.

"Let us sit down on it," said another girl, and she sat on it, the penis entering her vagina. Suddenly Napi thrust upward and the girl was killed.[147]

........................................................................................

*The Crow version combines two stories into one. In the first part, Old Man Coyote has his adventure with his strawberry penis, and in the second, he finds the girls, who are pretending to be dead. While he is checking them over, one farts in his face, and Old Man Coyote concludes they must have been dead a long time as they smelled so bad.*

# Napi and the Gophers

✿

Napi was wandering over the prairie when he saw a fire and decided to investigate. When he peered through some bushes, he saw some gophers sitting in a circle around the fire playing a game. As he watched, he saw how a gopher would lie down on the ground while the others covered him with hot ashes. After a little time he said, "*Sk, sk*" (like a gopher), at which time the others uncovered him and they all laughed together.

Napi wanted to join them, so he came out of the bushes and started to cry. When the gophers asked him why he was crying, he said he was lonesome. "Let me, too, sit by that fire," he begged.

The gophers said, "All right, Old Man, don't cry; come and sit by the fire." They made a place for him and he watched them having fun.

"Little brothers," he begged, "teach me how to do that."

"It is not difficult to do," they told him. "We squeal, then we throw each other out of the ashes."

Napi wanted to try, so he lay down and the gophers began piling hot ashes on him, but he was not even half covered when he gave a signal and they took the ashes off him. Then Napi said it was his turn to cover the gophers. At first he did them one at a time and they had great fun, but finally he said, "My brothers, it is too much trouble to bury every one of you separately. I shall bury you all at once."

A young pregnant gopher who stood to one side said to Napi, "Old Man, my elder brother, I should not be buried. My belly might burst from the fire."

And Napi replied, "Just go away, so that there will be some gophers from you in the future."

The rest of the gophers lay down in a row and Napi covered them all with a deep pile of hot ashes. After a few moments one of the gophers said, "*Sk, sk,*" but Napi took no notice of his cries. "*Sk, sk, sk, sk!*" More squeals came from the ashes, but Napi ignored them as they became fainter and fainter, and finally stopped.

Meanwhile, Napi went away and collected some red willow branches to make a plate. When he got back, all the gophers had been roasted, so he piled them together, scraped the hair off a few of them and began to eat. When he was full he lay down to have a nap, but before going to sleep he told his anus (Little Brown Eye) to keep watch so that no one would steal his gophers.

"Be careful," Napi said. "If someone comes, wake me up."

After a while Little Brown Eye saw a bird and so he made a noise (as only an anus can do). Napi jumped up and said, "What is it?"

"A raven is flying by, over there."

"That is nothing."

Napi was asleep again when Little Brown Eye made another noise. "What is it now?"

"There is a coyote over there, coming this way."

"A coyote is nothing," said Napi, bawling out his anus for bothering him. He went back to sleep.[148]

Napi was sound asleep when a bobcat crept into view. The anus saw him and made a noise, but Napi slept. Again and again the anus made a noise, but the Old Man didn't stir. The bobcat, seeing that Napi was asleep, began to feast on the roasted gophers, and when they were all eaten, he went away.

Napi awoke, and when he went to eat, he discovered that the gophers were gone. Looking around, he saw the bobcat's greasy footprints and easily followed its tracks. A short distance away, he found the animal asleep on a rock.

"I will teach you to steal my food," he said as he pounced on the frightened animal. He took him by the ears and stretched them long. He pulled out his nice long tail, leaving only a stubby end. Next he pounded the head against a rock to flatten his face, then stretched the hind legs and body to make them longer. Finally, he pulled the hair from the pubic area and stuck them into the bobcat's face for whiskers and tufts for his ears. He then picked up the bobcat and carried him back to his camp, where he threw him into the fire. The animal jumped free but his body was scorched, which is why bobcats are yellow today.

Because of this incident, the Blackfoot still call bobcats Nap-iyo, or Old Man Greasy Stepping. "You bobcats will always look like this," Napi said, "and you will always be so short-winded, that you will never be able to run far."

Still angry that his food had been stolen, Napi now turned his attention to Little Brown Eye. Angrily, he said, "Little Brown Eye, I told you to wake me up if anything came around. Here you let a [bobcat] eat all my meat." Little Brown Eye argued that he had tried to wake him up but Napi would not listen. He grabbed a burning silver willow stick from the fire and as punishment he rubbed it into Little Brown Eye. That is why, ever since, the silver willow has been called *otsipits*, or dirty wood.

Napi howled in pain after burning himself and ran up a hill, holding his anus towards the wind. He pleaded with the wind to blow harder and cool him down. The wind obliged, but it was not enough, so Napi begged it to blow even harder. The hard wind that came blew him off the hill to the creek called Birch Creek. Napi tried to catch weeds and brush to stop himself, but the wind was too strong. Finally, he grasped a birch tree, which did not give way, even though the wind whipped him this way and that, up and down.

When the wind calmed, Napi turned to the birch tree and said, "Here, you old birch-tree! You spoiled all my fun. I was having a fine time playing with the wind. We were running over the hills and the mountains and through the woods, until you caught hold of me. Now I am going to punish you." Napi took his flint knife and slashed the tree, making huge gashes in its bark. These marks are still visible today on the bark of a birch tree.[149]

.............................................................................................................

*Birch Creek in Montana takes its name from this event.*

*Grinnell "cleaned up" his version of the story by saying that it was Napi's nose, not his anus, that was supposed to have been on guard and*

was punished. Wissler and Duvall and McClintock say that the animals buried in the ashes were squirrels, not gophers, while Grinnell says they were rabbits. Also, Grinnell combines this story with the one of Napi racing a wounded wolf. Chumak considers the Stoney Nakoda story to be a continuation of the account of the trickster and the spruce hens.

Similar stories are told by the Apache, Gros Ventre, and Cheyenne. The Assiniboine and the Northern Saulteaux consider the race to be a continuation of the killing of the ducks. The Northern Saulteaux say the trickster burned his anus when it failed to warn him about the food thief, but the anus got revenge by farting every time the trickster was hunting and frightened away the game.[150]

# Napi and the Dancing Mice

---

One day, Napi was travelling about when he heard singing near a clump of rose bushes. Going over to investigate, he found a large elk skull, and inside, some mice were dancing and singing. The chief mouse started the dance by singing, "Mice, swing the eyes, penis hairs, many penis hairs." Then they all stood up and joined in the singing, taking hold of each other's paws and dancing in a circle. As he watched them, Napi began to cry until one of the mice was sent out to find out what was wrong.

Said Napi, "I want to join you."

The little mouse explained that the skull was just too small for him, so he should lie outside and join the singing from there. He did this for a few moments, but complained that he was still isolated and alone. "Well, Old Man, just put your head into the elk-head and shake it," said the mouse. He was told that bobbing his head up and down would be just like dancing. But the mouse warned him, "Don't sleep. While we are dancing, we don't sleep. If one goes to sleep while dancing, the hair of his head will be bitten off." The hair, explained the mouse, would be used to make soft linings for their nests.

As the night wore on Napi became sleepy, and towards morning he took a short nap. But the head mouse roused him and said, "Try hard, my elder brother, we have nearly done dancing."

Napi tried his best to stay awake, but the music, the singing, and the constant nodding of his head soon made him fall into a deep sleep.

By the time the dance ended, the mice had chewed off all his hair on his head.

When Napi awoke he was all alone and could see nothing except the inside of the skull. He tried to pull it off but it was stuck fast, so he wandered blindly out onto the prairie, the elk's two antlers branching out grotesquely from each side of his head. When Napi bumped into a tree, he asked it where it was standing. The tree said, "I am standing on a hill." The next two trees answered the same, and when he came to a fourth tree, it indicated it was standing near the edge of a coulee. Napi passed it, went down into the coulee, and walked along until he came to a fifth tree that was standing on the edge of a steep riverbank.

Napi asked this tree how far it was to the river and the tree, having no love for the trickster, told him that the river was far away. Napi's next step took him over the bank, and he fell headlong into the river. The water was deep and the current swift as it carried him out into the centre of the stream.

Napi floated along until he came to a camp. There he bellowed like a bull elk and when some women heard him they cried, "There comes an elk-bull swimming down the river." The men rushed out with the lariats and roped him, but when they pulled him ashore they discovered it was Napi and not an elk.

"That is the Old Man," they said. "I wonder whether there is something the matter with him, why he put that elk-head on his head." They tried to pull it off, but it was stuck fast. Finally, two old women took their stone axes and, standing on each side of him, hit the skull with two swift blows. The skull was smashed to pieces, but the triumph of the women turned to shock as the trickster's head came into view.

"Look at his head; he is crazy!" they shouted. "Run, run, he has no hair, he is crazy, he is dangerous!"

Later, when they realized that Napi wasn't a water monster, they all laughed and asked him why he was bald. "Oh," he said. "It is too hot, that's why I cut all my hair."[151]

*In a different version of this story, the mice were doing a war dance in a hole in the ground, beating drums and brandishing spears of grass. Napi joined them with just his head inside the hole. He was told that the first one to sleep would have their hair cut off. Napi showed them a new kind of dance, and when it was finished, all the mice had gone to sleep. Napi then took his knife and cut off their whiskers (or their pubic hairs). Similar stories are told by the Gros Ventre, Stoney Nakoda, and Assiniboine.*[152]

# The Old Women and the Babies

---⚜---

After the women had broken the elk skull that encased Napi's head, he told them he was hungry. Napi was always hungry. Two old women invited him to their place to eat.

When he saw how comfortable it was, he said, "If you want I can stay with you this winter and leave next summer. When there is no more meat I can hunt and you will always have something to eat." Each of the women had a baby. They agreed that Napi should stay for the winter and in spring he would look after them when their food was almost gone.

One day, Napi told the old women he was going deer hunting. When he was out in the woods he pulled some hair from his robe and rubbed his buttocks in the snow until they bled, leaving bloody marks in the snow. As soon as he got back to the lodge he told the women he had made a successful hunt. "Go on, go and get the carcass. Leave your children here. I shall watch them. Follow my trail. There in the forest you will find the black-tail deer that I killed." The women saw that he was bleeding and that his robe was torn, so they knew he must have put up a good fight.

The women harnessed their dogs and set off for the carcass. No sooner were they out of sight than Napi cut the heads off the two babies and put their bodies into a large pot to cook. He put the heads into their swings, then arranged the blankets to make it look as though they were sleeping.

The women came back some time later, saying, "We cannot find the meat. The snow was all bloody, with hair scattered around. The coyotes must have eaten it."

Napi told them not to worry. "While you were gone, I got an antelope. It is cooking in the pot. Now be careful; don't wake the babies. I shall go after some wood." Meanwhile, he told them to start eating.

Outside, Napi gathered wood and piled it in front of the lodge until the entrance was completely blocked. Then he called out to the women, "Your babies are cooking in the pot."

They ran over to the swings, pulled back the blankets, and were shocked when the two heads rolled out. Angrily, they rushed to the door, but it was blocked by the pile of firewood. They kicked it aside and soon were in pursuit of Napi, who was running down the trail. When he came to a coyote den, he dashed inside where the women were afraid to follow him.

As they sat weeping beside the den, Napi crept out of another exit and changed his appearance. When he came to them, he said, "Ah, old women, what are you doing, why do you sit crying?"

"It is the Old Man that killed our children, and he has run in here."

Napi said, "Oh, I hate the Old Man! I will go in there and kill him for you."

Napi went inside the hole where he shouted and made sounds of a terrible fight. At last, when everything was quiet, he came out of the hole and announced that Napi was dead. "I have killed him in there," he said. "You may prepare to pull him out, both of you."

Obediently, the women went into the den, but while they were inside, Napi built a big fire at the entrance and smothered them to death.

"It is not good that old women have children," he said.[153]

..............................................................................................

*In one version of this story, Napi left his anus hanging from a tree, where the old women found it. They took it home, but after they cooked it, whenever they tried to chew it, the meat simply farted. A similar story is told by the Gros Ventre.*[154]

## Napi and the Ducks

One day, Napi was walking along the river with his brother Beaver and saw a number of ducks swimming nearby. Always hungry, Napi sent his brother to dive under the water and find the ones with the fattest legs. He then told him to pull them under the water and drown them. Thus, Napi had enough food to last him for months.

By autumn he was hungry again, so he looked for large flocks of ducks flying south for the winter. He hailed them as they flew overhead, telling them how warm the water was in the river. However, the water was ice cold, and when they landed, their legs were quickly frozen in the ice. When he was done, Napi had enough food to last him for the winter.[155]

*An almost identical version of this story is told by the Assiniboine. In a Stoney Nakoda version, the birds were spruce grouse.*[156]

# The Great Marriage

---  ❄  ---

One day, Napi was hunting when he came to the banks of the Highwood River, and there in the distance, he saw a number of tipis of magnificent workmanship. This is when he first discovered that the woman who had separated from him after the death of the child had created women, just as he had created men. They had made their lodges of the finest cowhide that glistened white in the sun, and everything about their camp was neat, clean, and tidy. Their leader had taught these women how to find all kinds of berries and how to make bags for them, how to preserve and prepare the berries, and how to harvest other food.

The men had been taught none of these skills. Their lodges were made from the backs of buffalo bull hide thrown over some poles, their clothes were shabby with pieces of dried meat still hanging from them, their moccasins were made of skin from the legs of the buffalo, and their food was coarse and poorly cooked. They loved to hunt and kill buffalo in the pound in a nearby creek, but they had no talent for cooking or dressing hides.

When Napi approached the strange camp, he began to shout and wave to attract the attention of the people. To his amazement, the camp was made up entirely of women who looked at him with curiosity. There was one lodge that was larger and more impressive than the rest, so Napi went inside, and there he met the chief, a beautiful woman wearing a doeskin dress richly ornamented with porcupine quills.

"I have created many men who are without companions," Napi explained. "Let us align my men on the bank of the river, and then your women can select husbands." When the women in the camp learned that they would no longer need to drive buffalo over the jump but could cook, sew, and tend to their lodges, they were very pleased.

The chief woman was agreeable and asked Napi, "How many chiefs are there in that tribe?"

He answered, "There are four chiefs. But the real chief of all the tribe you will know when you see him by this—he is finely dressed and wears a robe trimmed and painted red, and carries a lance with a bone head on each end." In fact, these were the clothes that Napi had intended to wear, as he wanted the woman chief as his wife.

"Go home," the woman told Napi, "bring all your men; stand them all on the top of this stone ridge; our women shall then go up one by one, and each take a man for a husband."

Napi went to the men's camp and told them what he had learned. He said that they would no longer have to cook or dress hides, for the women would do that. All they would have to do was to hunt and bring food to the camp.

The following day, the men travelled northward until they came to the women's camp. Obediently, they stood in a line on the hill and waited for the women to choose their husbands.

The woman chief said to her companions, "I shall take my choice from them. When I come back, you will go up one by one. Now we will take husbands."

She had been busy making dried meat, so she was dirty and her hands, arms, and clothing were covered with blood and grease. She did not change but made straight for the man wearing a wolf robe trimmed and painted red. She took him by the hand to lead him away but Napi pulled back and said to her, "No. Go away, you dirty old woman. I will not marry you."

Angrily, the woman went back to her lodge and reemerged in her finest clothing. Napi did not recognize her and cried, "Oh, what a fine woman. How I would like to marry her."

Without hesitation, the chief woman walked up to Napi and he was convinced that she was going to choose him, but she went right past him and picked the man next to him. Then, as Napi stood dumbfounded, she announced to the women, "Each of you choose a husband, but let none take Napi, he of the wolf clothes; he refused me when I was in rags and dirt and now he will remain single." As the women came forward, Napi walked in front of them, but they just ignored him and picked someone else. At last, all the women had chosen their mates and Napi stood alone on the hill.

Shaking her fist at him, the chief woman said, "You have made me ashamed in the eyes of all the other women by not coming with me when I chose you for a husband. Now you will remain standing on that spot, but not as Napi, for I will prepare a charm which will turn you into a pine tree."

And she did.[157]

---

*Each storyteller has a different description of Napi and the clothing he wore for this occasion. Uhlenbeck says he was very tall. R.N. Wilson says he wore a suit of wolf fur; Little Chief says a buffalo calf robe, buffalo hide leggings, and a buffalo hide fur cap; Hale, leggings trimmed with weasel skin; Lowie, a wolf robe with the tail on; and White Bull, an eagle feather on the back of his head standing up.*

*According to Uhlenbeck, before they met the women, the men also did not know how to build lodges, tan buffalo hides, cut dried meat, or make their own clothes. And Wilson attributed the women's education in these things and more to Napi, rather than the women's leader.*

*This tale is the basis for the name of two sites in the Alberta foothills. The women's buffalo jump is Akipiskun, west of Cayley, on Squaw Coulee. About forty kilometres south is the men's buffalo jump, Ninapiskun, west of Nanton. John Yellowhorn, a Peigan chief, remembered seeing a pine tree still standing by the buffalo jump when his family passed by there* when he was a child. Joe Little Chief wrote, "The first pine tree was old so another would grow in its place. To-day you can see that pine tree and that is Napew when he turned into a pine tree for being so smart. To-day a lot of tribes go and see that place, it is called Woman's Buffalo Trap. It is well known to all tribes."[158]

Some storytellers believe the Napi accounts should end here. As Jim White Bull says, now that men and women were getting married, they would make their own children and there was no longer a need for Napi to create anything. However, other stories have persisted about families well beyond the wedding incident. It is possible, however, that these later incidents may have involved animals, rather than humans, or were borrowed from Coyote trickster tales from other tribes that had no wedding ceremony.

The Stoney Nakoda are the only other tribe that seem to have an account of the wedding story, although it is obviously a derivative of the Blackfoot story. In their version, even the site of the marriage was the same, "near Porcupine Hills and Old-Man River."[159] However, the Stoney account has a prologue, beginning with the trickster and the woman hunting buffalo together and the woman learning from him about sexual intercourse.

# Napi and His Mother-in-Law

---

Napi was camped with his wife and mother-in-law. One day, he went away and began to make tracks as though many people had gone by. Farther along, he pitched a number of tipi poles that looked like a deserted camp. When he returned, he sat around and said nothing for a long time.

At last his wife asked, "Is there anything the matter with you that you do not speak?"

He replied, "I wish very much to be with those people who went to war with their mothers-in-law. They all went to the war."

He showed her the tracks and said that on the other side of the creek was the place where they all camped. He begged that his mother-in-law go to war with him so that he might join the others and she agreed.

He went with her to the other side of the creek and when they got to the tipi poles he said, "They must have gone away, those who went to war. Let us sleep here tonight."

They were bedded down for a short time when Napi began to cry as if he was freezing.

"Napi, are you cold?" asked his mother-in-law.

"Yes, I am very cold. Let us sleep together. I shall sleep warm if you sleep with me."

She agreed, and they slept together. That night he had sexual intercourse with her, and in the morning he said, "Let us go back."

So they went back home.[160]

*This is an unlikely Blackfoot story. Napi was a loner and on the few occasions when he had company, it was usually a kit fox or other animal. Rather, this story has probably been borrowed from another tribe where the trickster had a wife and family. The story was known to the Gros Ventre, Arapaho, and Crow. Among the Gros Ventre, the story is basically the same but contains more detail about the trickster's sexual activity (published in Latin in Victorian style). In the Crow account, Old Man Coyote tricks the mother-in-law into disrobing when crossing a stream and that night makes her believe she had to sleep with him or he would die. It ends with the lesson, "This must be why women do not tell what they have done."*[161]

## Napi and the Wolves

───────────────── ❀ ─────────────────

Now Napi was walking along, and far off he saw a pack of wolves gathered around their chief. He admired the strong handsome animals, so he went to their chief and cried, "Pity me, Wolf Chief; make me into a wolf, that I may live your way and catch deer and everything that runs fast."

"Come near then," said the Wolf Chief, "that I may rub your body with my hands, so that hair will cover you."

But Napi did not want his entire body covered. "Hold," he said, "do not cover my body with hair. On my head, arms, and legs only."

Wolf Chief obliged and then offered to give Napi three companions who would teach him how to hunt like a wolf. "One is a swift runner," he said, "another a good runner, and the last is not very fast. Take them with you now, and others of my younger children who are learning to hunt, but do not go to where the wind blows; keep in the shelter, or the young ones will freeze to death."

As usual, Napi paid no attention to the good advice given to him, but went directly to the high buttes where the wind was blowing and the temperature cold. That night he nearly froze and called to the young wolves, "Cover me with your tails." So all the little ones crowded around him and covered him with their tails. After a while he awoke because of the warmth and angrily said, "Take off those tails!" and hurriedly the wolves all moved away from him. But Napi soon became cold again and this time he pleaded with the wolves, "Oh, my young brothers, cover me with your tails or I shall freeze." And so it was that the obliging young wolves returned to Napi's side.

Next morning, the three old wolves took Napi and the young ones to show them how to hunt. The first animals they saw were a number of moose, so they gave chase and killed three. Then, just as they were going to eat, Wolf Chief arrived with his retinue and announced that they would make pemmican for the winter. Napi had to obey, but he wanted to eat immediately.

The pemmican maker warned, "No one must look, everybody shut his eyes, while I make the pemmican." But Napi looked, so the wolf threw a round bone at him that struck him on the nose. This made Napi angry, so he said that he would make his own pemmican and told everyone to close their eyes. He then took the round bone and beat the pemmican maker to death.

"Why did you kill your brother?" demanded Wolf Chief.

"I didn't mean to," lied Napi. "He looked and I threw the round bone at him, but I only meant to hurt him a little."

Said the wolf, "You cannot live with us any longer. Take one of your companions and go off by yourselves and hunt."

Napi chose the swift runner to be his partner, and so they went to live by themselves. They killed plenty of elk, deer, and moose, and for once Napi had plenty to eat.

Then one morning Napi woke up and told the swift runner that he had had a bad dream. "Hereafter," he warned, "when you chase anything, if it jumps a stream, you must not follow it. Even a little spring you must not jump."

That day while out hunting, the swift runner chased a moose that ran across a tiny stream and onto a small island. "This is such a little stream," the wolf thought, "that I must jump it. That moose is very tired, and I don't think it will leave the island." But as soon as he jumped over the stream the wolf was attacked and killed by a bear. He had had no way of knowing that the island was the home of Bear Chief and his two brothers.

When the wolf did not return to camp, Napi set out to find him. He asked all the birds he met if they had seen the swift runner, but they had not. At last he came to a kingfisher that was sitting on a limb overlooking the stream.

"Why do you sit there, my young brother?"

"Because the Bear Chief and his brothers have killed your wolf; they have eaten the meat and thrown the fat into the river, and whenever I see a piece come floating along, I fly down and get it."

Napi enquired about the bears and was told that they lived on the island and came out every morning to play. Napi saw their tracks where they had been playing, so he turned himself into a rotten tree nearby and waited for them. Next morning, the Bear Chief was the first on the scene. When he saw the tree he said to his brothers, "Look at that rotten tree. It is Old Man. Go, brothers, and see if it is not."

The two brothers looked at the tree and clawed it. "No," they said, "it is only a tree." The Bear Chief went over and he too clawed it and bit it. Napi, although hurt, never moved. This convinced the bears this was only a tree, so they started to play. Then, while they had their backs to him, Napi shot an arrow into each of them. Although deadly in their aim, none of the arrows killed the bears as they fled into the interior of the island.

Napi reverted to his original form, and was walking beside the stream when he saw a frog leaping about and singing, "Chief Bear! Chief Bear! Napi kill him, Chief Bear! Napi kill him, Chief Bear!"[162]

"What do you say?" said Napi. "Tell me about it."

The frog told how Napi had turned himself into a rotten tree and then shot the bears. "They are not dead," said the frog, "but the arrows are very near their hearts; if you should shove ever so little on them, the points would cut their hearts." The frog added that the bears had sent him to get medicine that would cure them.

Napi killed the frog, skinned it, and covered himself with its hide. He then crossed to the island, singing just as the frog had done.

"Hurry," said the Bear Chief impatiently. Napi hopped up to the bear and shoved the arrow in until it pierced his heart. As he slumped down, Napi told the brothers, "I cured him; he is asleep now." Then each of the brothers died in the same way.

Napi built a huge fire, skinned the bears, and rendered their fat in a hollow he made in the ground. He called for all the animals to come and roll in it. The bears came first, which is why they are so fat. Last came the rabbits, but by this time the fat was almost gone. All they could do was to dip their paws into the remaining fat and rub it on their backs and between their hind legs. That is why rabbits have two such large layers of fat in those places.

"I have done some good," concluded Napi. "I have avenged the death of my wolf partner and have made fat many of my younger brothers."[163]

........................................................................................

*As Grinnell notes, this story shows "the serious side of Old Man's character."[164] In one version of the story, there are only two wolves, Long Body and Heavy Body. Napi killed Long Body, presumably the pemmican-maker in Grinnell's account, and saw Heavy Body killed by the bears. In a Cree version of this story, the trickster Wisûkejak ordered the young wolves to move their tails from him because they kept farting.[165]*

# Napi and the Snakes

Napi was walking alone one day when he saw three lodges. As he approached them, he saw that each had a guard outside. He went to the first lodge but was warned by the guard that there was a dangerous snake inside. But Napi, as usual, did not listen, and went inside. There he saw a huge snake lying in the middle of the lodge.

When it didn't move, Napi poked it with his flint knife and asked it if it was going to get up.

Aroused, the snake immediately coiled up, ready to strike the trickster.

"You'd better get out before I eat you up," it hissed.

Heeding the warning, Napi left the lodge and went to the next one. There, too, the guard told him to go away and again Napi did not listen. When he went into the second lodge, he found another huge snake asleep; when he poked it with his knife, it also threatened to kill him.

Still curious, Napi went to the third lodge. The guard told him to go away, but instead Napi went inside. This time there was no snake, only twenty hearts lying on the ground. When he asked the guard what this meant, the guard said, "These are hearts of twenty eagles who have been catching people and eating them."

Napi poked one of the hearts with his knife and somewhere an eagle dropped dead. One by one Napi stabbed the hearts, and when he was finished, all the eagles were dead and would no longer prey on their helpless victims.[166]

*This is probably not a Napi story, but rather a tale borrowed from another tribe and attributed to the trickster.*

# NOTES

## INTRODUCTION

1  Walter McClintock, *The Old North Trail, Or, Life, Legends, and Religion of the Blackfeet Indians* (Lincoln, NB: University of Nebraska Press, 1999), 338.

2  In the stories, Napi is given a variety of names, including Kenuk-akkatsis (Surrounded by All) by the North Peigans and Mikohkkayew (Man Who Wears a Short Red Robe) by the Blackfoot. The South Peigans called him Painted Dried Meat, or Fooled a Little (meaning the opposite). Other names were Omark-oummapiw (Large Space Where a Lodge Once Stood), Aka-etsikin (Old Moccasins), Apekan-etsikin (Moccasins Made from Badly Tanned Leather), Omark-etsikin (Big Moccasins), and Makok'im (Old Lodge Cover).

3  Clark Wissler and David C. Duvall, *Mythology of the Blackfoot Indians* (New York: American Museum of Natural History, 1908), 9.

4  Walter McClintock, *Old Indian Trails* (Boston: Houghton Mifflin, 1923), 171.

5  George Bird Grinnell, *Blackfood Lodge Tales* (Lincoln: University of Nebraska Press, 1962), 162.

6  Wissler and Duvall, *Mythology of the Blackfoot Indians*, 17.

7  See John Nelson, "Blackfoot Names of a Number of Places in the North-West Territory, for the Most Part in the Vicinity of the Rocky Mountains," *Report of Progress, 1882-83-84.* Ottawa: Geological and Natural History Survey and Museum of Canada, Appendix II, Nelson, 1885, 161.

8  Nelson, "Blackfoot Names," 162.

9  Ibid., 161.

10  Wissler and Duvall, *Mythology of the Blackfoot Indians*, 28, n2.

11   Mike Mountain Horse, *My People the Bloods* (Calgary: Glenbow-Alberta Institute and Blood Tribal Council, 1979), 83.

12   Richard G. Forbis, *The Old Women's Buffalo Jump, Alberta*, Bulletin No. 180 (Ottawa: National Museum of Canada, 1960), 58.

13   Interview, Hugh Dempsey with John Cotton, January 4, 1957, James Gladstone interpreting. In Forbis, *Old Women's Buffalo Jump*, 61.

14   Dagmar Siebelt, *Die Winter Counts der Blackfoot* (Munster, Germany: Lit Verlag, 2005), 362.

15   Robert N. Wilson, *The R.N. Wilson Papers*, vol. 1, ed. Philip H. Godsell (Calgary: Glenbow Foundation, 1958), 28.

16   Horatio Hale, "Report on the Blackfoot Tribes" (London: British Association of the Advancement of Science, 1885), 705.

17   J.L. Levern, "Notes et Souvenirs Concernant les Piednoirs," manuscript, Microfilm No. 234, Glenbow Archives, Calgary.

18   Wissler and Duvall, *Mythology of the Blackfoot Indians*, 23.

19   John Maclean, "Blackfoot Mythology," *Journal of American Folk-Lore*, 6, no. 22 (July-September 1893): 168.

20   Other creatures mentioned include the osprey, loon, and badger.

21   George Bird Grinnell, *Blackfoot Lodge Tales: The Story of a Prairie People* (New York: Charles Scribner's Sons, 1892), 272–74.

22   Grinnell, *Blackfoot Lodge Tales*, 257.

23   Levern, "Notes."

24   Grinnell, *Blackfoot Lodge Tales*, 257–58.

25   Wissler and Duvall, *Mythology of the Blackfoot Indians*, 19.

26   "The Religion of the Blackfeet Indians, as told by Richard Sanderville," Anthropological Archives, Smithsonian Institution, June 30, 1934, File 4080 Blackfoot.

27   Wilson, *Wilson Papers*, 48–51; Grinnell, *Blackfoot Lodge Tales*, 145–46; Cecil Black Plume, "Adventures of Napi," *The Outlook* (Lethbridge), December 1972.

28   In Grinnell (*Blackfoot Lodge Tales*, 46), the child who found them was a boy.

29   Wilson says Napi turned himself into a buffalo bull (*Wilson Papers*, 51).

30   Wilson, *Wilson Papers*, 51.

31   Peter Fidler, "Journal of a Journey over Land from Buckingham House to the Rocky Mountains in 1792 & 3," Hudson's Bay Company Archives, E.3/2, Provincial Archives of Manitoba.

32   McClintock, *The Old North Trail*, 382–93.

33   Elliott Coues, Alexander Henry, and David Thompson, *New Light on the Early History of the Greater Northwest: The Manuscript Journals of Alexander Henry and of David Thompson, 1799–1814* (New York: Francis P. Harper, 1897), 527–28.

34   Letter, James Doty to Isaac Stevens, December 24, 1854, Records of the Bureau of Indian Affairs, Washington Superintendency, Field Papers, Letters received from Eastern District. U.S. National Archives, Washington, DC.

35   Letter by Lacombe published in Émile Petitot, *Traditions indiennes du Canada nord-ouest,* Part 7: *Légendes et traditions des Pieds-Noirs au Canada* (Paris: Maisonneuve frères et C. Leclerc, 1886), 500–4.

36   Cited in Hale, "Report on the Blackfoot Tribes," 705.

37   Ibid., 704.

38   Petitot, *Traditions indiennes*, 495–96.

39   E.F. Wilson, "Report on the Blackfoot Tribes." Report of the British Association for the Advancement of Science 57 (1887): 185.

40   Maclean, "Blackfoot Mythology," 165–72.

41   Ibid., 165.

42   Ibid.

43   Grinnell, *Blackfoot Lodge Tales* (1892).

44   George Bird Grinnell, *Blackfeet Indian Stories* (New York: Charles Scribner's Sons, 1913).

45   Included are French translations of stories written in the Blackfoot language by Émile Legal.

46   Wissler and Duvall, *Mythology of the Blackfoot Indians*; Christianus C. Uhlenbeck, *Original Blackfoot Texts* (Amsterdam: Johannes Müller, 1911); Christianus C. Uhlenbeck, *A New Series of Blackfoot Texts* (Amsterdam: Johannes Müller, 1912); and Jan Petrus Benjamin de Josselin de Jong, *Blackfoot Texts from the Southern Peigans Blackfoot Reservation, Teton County, Montana* (Amsterdam: Johannes Müller, 1914).

47    De Jong, *Blackfoot Texts*, 2.

48    Unpublished papers in author's files, Calgary.

49    Joe Little Chief's Blackfoot Stories, M-4394, in Joe Little Chief fonds, Glenbow Archives, Calgary.

50    Mountain Horse, *My People*.

51    Darnell Davis Rides at the Door, *Napi Stories* (Browning, MT: Blackfeet Heritage Program, 1979).

52    Black Plume, "Adventures of Napi."

53    Frances Fraser, *The Bear Who Stole the Chinook* (Toronto: Macmillan, 1959) and *The Wind Along the River* (Toronto: Macmillan, 1968).

54    Blackfeet Community Education Program, *Blackfeet Cook Book* (Browning, MT: Blackfeet Community Education Program, 1969).

55    Percy Bullchild, *The Sun Came Down: The History of the World as My Blackfeet Elders Told It* (San Francisco: Harper and Row, 1985).

56    Ibid., 269.

57    Sebastian Chumak, *The Stonies of Alberta: An Illustrated Heritage of Genesis, Myths, Legends, Folklore and Wisdom of Wichastabi, the People-Who-Cook-With-Hot-Stones* (Calgary: The Alberta Foundation, 1983) and *The Wisdom of the Blackfoot, the Bloods and the Peigans of Canada* (Toronto: Canada Heritage Foundation, 1988).

58    Chumak, *The Wisdom of the Blackfoot*, 128.

59    Ibid., 100.

60    Ibid., 132.

61    Ibid., 85.

62    Frank Bird Linderman, *Old Man Coyote* (New York, John Day Company, 1931), 214–15.

63    Chumak, *The Wisdom of the Blackfoot*, 62, 64.

64    Rick Tailfeathers, "How the Mice Saved Christmas," *Kainai News* (southern Alberta), December 1-2, 1980, 28.

65    See Wissler and Duvall, "The Seven Stars," in *Mythology of the Blackfoot Indians*, 68–72.

66 Ruth Little Bear, "Indian Version of the Creation," *Kainai News*, June 5, 1968.

67 In a variation of this story, the children of the Sun and Moon were Napi and Morning Star. This account has no Christian content. See Richard Sanderville, "The Religion of the Blackfeet Indians," 1934, file 4080, Anthropological Archives, Smithsonian Institution, Washington, DC.

68 Uhlenbeck, "Bear-Chief's Cosmology," in *Original Blackfoot Texts*, 91–93.

69 Interview with Robert Many Heads, South Peigan, by Claude Schaeffer, November 20, 1951 (Schaeffer papers, Glenbow Archives).

70 Wissler and Duvall, "Scar Face," in *Mythology of the Blackfoot Indians*, 61–65, and "Elk Woman," 83–85.

71 Wissler and Duvall, "Old Man and the Great Spirit," in *Mythology of the Blackfoot Indians*, 23–24.

72 Wilson, "Notes by Mr. H. Hale on the Report of the Rev. E.F. Wilson," *Report on the North-West Indian Tribes of Canada*, British Association for the Advancement of Science, 1887.

73 Interview with Pete Standing Alone, July 18, 2009; Rides at the Door, 1979, 7.

74 De Jong, *Blackfoot Texts*, 2.

75 Uhlenbeck, *A New Series of Blackfoot Texts*, 184.

76 Ibid., 196.

77 De Jong, *Blackfoot Texts*, 5, 73.

78 Wissler and Duvall, *Mythology of the Blackfoot Indians*, 5.

79 Rides at the Door, *Napi Stories*, 7.

80 Wissler and Duvall, *Mythology of the Blackfoot Indians*, 5.

81 Grinnell, *Blackfeet Indian Stories*, 148.

82 Levern, "Notes."

83 Barry Holstun Lopez, *Giving Birth to Thunder, Sleeping with his Daughter: Coyote Builds North America* (New York: Avon Books, 1977), 62, 75.

84 A.L. Kroeber, *Gros Ventre Myths and Tales* (New York: American Museum of Natural History, 1907), 69–70.

85  Richard Erdoes and Alfonso Ortiz, eds., *American Indian Myths and Legends* (New York: Pantheon Books, 1984), 338–39.

86  Robert H. Lowie, "The Northern Cheyenne," undated typescript, Glenbow Museum Archives.

87  Pliny Earle Goddard, *Apache Texts*, Anthropological Papers of the American Museum of History, vol. 8 (New York: Published by Order of the Trustees, 1911), 234.

88  Robert H. Lowie, *The Assiniboine* (New York: American Museum of Natural History, 1909), 108.

89  Chumak, *The Stonies of Alberta*, 88.

90  Rodney Frey, *Stories that Make the World: Oral Literature of the Indian Peoples of the Inland Northwest* (Norman: University of Oklahoma Press, 1995), 71–75.

91  Edna Kenton, ed., *The Jesuit Relations and Allied Documents: Travels and Explorations of the Jesuit Missionaries in North America (1610–1791)* (New York: Vanguard Press, 1954).

92  Joseph François Lafitau, *Customs of the American Indians Compared with the Customs of Primitive Times* (Toronto: The Champlain Society, 1974), vol. 1, 86.

93  Paul Radin, *The Trickster: A Study in Native American Mythology* (New York: Schocken Books, 1972), xxiii.

94  Claude Lévi-Strauss, "Structuralism and Ecology," in *Readings for a History of Anthropological Theory*, ed. Paul A. Erickson and Liam Donat Murphy (Toronto: University of Toronto Press, 2013), 167.

95  Carl G. Jung, *Four Archetypes: Mother, Rebirth, Spirit, Trickster* (Princeton: Princeton University Press, 1970).

96  Cited in Michael P. Carroll, "Levi-Strauss, Freud, and the Trickster: A New Perspective upon an Old Problem," *American Ethnologist*, 8, no. 2 (May 1981): 311.

97  Barbara Babcock-Abrahams, "'A Tolerated Margin of Mess': The Trickster and his Tales Reconsidered," *Journal of the Folklore Institute*, 11, no. 3 (1975): 161. Cited by Franchot Ballinger, "Living Sideways: Social Themes and Social Relationships in Native American Trickster Tales," *American Indian Quarterly*, 13, no. 1 (Winter 1989): 15.

98  Esther S. Goldfrank, "'Old Man' and the Father Image in Blood (Blackfoot) Society," in *Psychoanalysis and Culture*, ed. G.B Wilbur and W. Muensterberger (New York: International Universities Press, 1951), 152.

99    Michael P. Carroll, "Lévi-Strauss, Freud, and the Trickster: A New Perspective upon an Old Problem," *American Ethnologist*, 8, no. 2 (May 1981): 310; Michael P. Carroll, "The Trickster as Selfish-Buffoon and Culture Hero," *Ethos*, 12, no. 2 (Summer 1984): 106.

100   Ibid.

101   Daniel G. Brinton, *Myths of the New World: A Treatise on the Symbolism and Mythology of the Red Race of America* (Philadelphia: David McKay, 1896), 194.

102   Franz Boas, *Traditions of the Thompson River Indians of British Columbia*. New York: Houghton Mifflin, 1898, 109.

103   Mac Linscott Ricketts, "The North American Indian Trickster," *History of Religions*, 5, no. 2 (Winter, 1966): 327–50.

104   Sigmund Freud, *Totem and Taboo: Resemblances between the Psychic Lives of Savages and Neurotics* (New York: Random House, 1918).

105   Carroll, "The Trickster as Selfish-Buffoon and Culture Hero," 306–7.

106   Levern, "Notes," 70.

## NAPI STORIES

107   Some say he began his adventures in the present Wyoming.

108   The Knees are located in central Montana.

109   Relayed by an elder in John C. Ewers, *The Horse in Blackfoot Indian Culture, with Comparative Material from Other Western Tribes* (Washington, DC: US Government Printing Office, 1955).

110   Levern, "Notes."

111   After hearing this part of the story, Hale ("Report," 705), concluded "that all the evil in the earth comes from the woman's contractious will." Levern picked up on this part of the story too, commenting that "by the strong will of the woman all is in the worst possible state in this world."

112   This story is compiled from Levern, "Notes," 58; Mountain Horse, *My People*, 111–12; Grinnell, *Blackfoot Lodge Tales*, 137–140; Wilson, *Wilson Papers*, 22, 53–54, 65; Jim White Bull, "The History of Great Temuelites or Blackfoot Nation. Their Indian God Old Man—Na-pee" (unpublished manuscript); Wissler and Duvall, *Mythology of the Blackfoot Indians*, 19–21; Hale, "Report," 705; Fraser Taylor, *Standing Alone:*

*A Contemporary Blackfoot Indian* (Halfmoon Bay, BC: Arbutus Bay Publications, 1989); and Maclean, "Blackfoot Mythology," 165.

113 Wilson, *Wilson Papers*, 22.

114 The implication of this is that the coyote was walking upright, not on all fours.

115 This story is compiled from Joe Little Chief, "History of the Blackfeet," 13, 36, 48, and "Late White Eagle," 10, in Joe Little Chief fonds, Glenbow Museum Archives; Uhlenbeck, *Original Blackfoot Texts*, 171; Wissler and Duvall, *Mythology of the Blackfoot Indians*, 28–29; Grinnell, *Blackfoot Lodge Tales*, 158; Maclean, "Blackfoot Mythology," 171; and Wilson, *Wilson Papers*, 26–28.

116 Chumak, *The Stonies*, 80.

117 This story is compiled from Uhlenbeck, *A New Series*, 187–88; White Bull, "The History," 1–2; Wilson, *Wilson Papers*, 29–30; Maclean, "Blackfoot Mythology," 170; Wissler and Duvall, *Mythology of the Blackfoot Indians*, 25.

118 Chumak, *The Stonies*, 74; Robert H. Lowie, *The Northern Shoshone* (New York: American Museum of Natural History, 1909), 120; George A. Dorsey, *The Pawnee Mythology* (Carnegie Institution of Washington, pub. 59, 446, No. 126. Washington, DC, 1904), 65; Erdoes and Ortiz, *American Indian Myths*, 337–39; Goddard, *Apache Texts*, 234.

119 This story is compiled from White Bull, "The History," 4; Grinnell, *Blackfoot Lodge Tales*, 167–68; Wissler and Duvall, *Mythology of the Blackfoot Indians*, 31–32; de Jong, *Blackfoot Texts*, 7–9; Wilson, *Wilson Papers*, 51–53; and Grinnell, *Blackfeet Indian Stories*, 174.

120 Erdoes and Ortiz, *American Indian Myths*, 162–63; Chumak, *The Stonies*, 74; Leonard Bloomfield, *Sacred Legends of the Sweet Grass Cree*, Bulletin No. 60 (Ottawa: National Museum of Canada, 1930), 55.

121 Uhlenbeck, *A New Series*, 188–91; Grinnell, *Blackfoot Lodge Tales*, 169–70; Wissler and Duvall, *Mythology of the Blackfoot Indians*, 36–37.

122 Chumak, *Wisdom of the Blackfoot*, 48.

123 This story is compiled from R.N. Wilson, *Wilson Papers*, 41; de Jong, *Blackfoot Texts*, 72; and Uhlenbeck, *A New Series*, 177–78.

124 This story is compiled from de Jong, *Blackfoot Texts*, 75; Uhlenbeck, *A New Series*, 183, and Wilson, *Wilson Papers*, 54–55.

125 Kroeber, *Gros Ventre Myths*, 75.

126 This story is compiled from Wissler and Duvall, *Mythology of the Blackfoot Indians*, 32, and Grinnell, *Blackfeet Indian Stories*, 167–68.

127 Grinnell, *Blackfeet Indian Stories*, 167.

128 This story is compiled from Grinnell, *Blackfeet Indian Stories*, 171, and de Jong, *Blackfoot Texts*, 5.

129 George A. Dorsey and A. L. Kroeber, *Traditions of the Arapaho* (vol. 101, no. 49. Chicago: Field Museum, Anthropological Publications, 1903), 66; Kroeber, *Gros Ventre Myths*, 70–71; Lowie, *The Northern Shoshone*, 109, 122; Goddard, *Apache Texts*, 230; Radin, *The Trickster*, 80; Grinnell, *Blackfoot Lodge Tales* (1962), 282; and Alanson Skinner, "Plains Cree Tales," *Journal of American Folk-Lore*, 29 (1916): 359.

130 This story is compiled from Uhlenbeck, *A New Series*, 182; Wilson, *Wilson Papers*, 36–38; and de Jong, *Blackfoot Texts*, 73–74.

131 Grinnell, *Blackfoot Lodge Tales* (1962), 283; Goddard, *Apache Texts*, 234; and Kroeber, *Gros Ventre Myths*, 69–70.

132 White Bull, "The History," 3.

133 The story recorded here is compiled from White Bull, "The History," 3–5; Grinnell, *Blackfeet Indian Stories*, 158; de Jong, *Blackfoot Texts*, 21; Black Plume, "Adventures of Napi"; de Jong, *Blackfoot Texts*, 22; Wilson, *Wilson Papers*, 38–41; Uhlenbeck, *A New Series*, 198; and Wissler and Duvall, *Mythology of the Blackfoot Indians*, 30.

134 Wilson, *Wilson Papers*, 38; Wissler and Duvall, *Mythology of the Blackfoot Indians*, 30; Black Plume, "Adventures of Napi"; Uhlenbeck, *A New Series*, 196; Kroeber, *Gros Ventre Myths*, 70; Erdoes and Ortiz, *American Indian Myths*, 381; Lowie, *The Assiniboine*, 117–19; Goddard, *Apache Texts*, 73; and George Bird Grinnell, *By Cheyenne Campfires* (Norman: University of Oklahoma Press, 1971), 294.

135 This story is compiled from Wissler and Duvall, *Mythology of the Blackfoot Indians*, 35–36; White Bull, "The History," 5–6; and Wilson, *Wilson Papers*, 43.

136 This story is compiled from McClintock, *The Old North Trail*, 343–44.

137 Ibid., 343–33; Chumak, *The Stonies*, 76.

138 Lowie, *The Assiniboine*, 107.

139 Ibid., 108.

140 This story is adapted from Grinnell, *Blackfeet Indian Stories*, 185, and other sources.

141 Walter James Hoffman, *The Menomini Indians* (Washington, DC: Bureau of American Ethnology, 1896), 54–55; Skinner, "Plains Cree Tales," 349; Alanson

Skinner, *Notes on the Eastern Cree and Northern Saulteaux* (New York: American Museum of Natural History, 1911), 84; Kroeber, *Gros Ventre Myths*, 71.

142 This story is compiled from de Jong, *Blackfoot Texts*, 72; Levern, "Notes"; Wilson, *Wilson Papers*, 55–56; and Lowie, *The Assiniboine*, 111.

143 This story is compiled from Grinnell, *Blackfoot Lodge Tales*, 159–63; Wilson, *Wilson Papers*, 43–46; de Jong, *Blackfoot Texts*, 25; and Wissler and Duvall, *Mythology of the Blackfoot Indians*, 34.

144 This story is compiled from Uhlenbeck, *A New Series*, 170; de Jong, *Blackfoot Texts*, 29–31, 71; McClintock, *The Old North Trail*, 498; and Wilson, *Wilson Papers*, 55.

145 This story is compiled from de Jong, *Blackfoot Texts*, 19; Wissler and Duvall, *Mythology of the Blackfoot Indians*, 36; Wilson, *Wilson Papers*, 42–43; Lowie, *The Assiniboine*, 119; and Skinner, "Plains Cree Tales," 351.

146 Wissler and Duvall, *Mythology of the Blackfoot Indians*, 36.

147 This story is compiled from Wissler and Duvall, *Mythology of the Blackfoot Indians*, 36; de Jong, *Blackfoot Texts*, 23; and Erdoes and Ortiz, *American Indian Myths*, 314.

148 Grinnell, *Blackfeet Indian Stories*, 181–82.

149 Uhlenbeck, *A New Series*, 176; Grinnell, *Blackfoot Lodge Tales*, 171–72, 177; McClintock, *The Old North Trail*, 183; Grinnell, *Blackfeet Indian Stories*, 180–85; Wissler and Duvall, *Mythology of the Blackfoot Indians*, 26–27; Grinnell, *Blackfeet Indian Stories*, 160–61; and Chumak, *The Stonies*, 80.

150 Chumak, *The Stonies*, 80; Goddard, *Apache Texts*, 230; Kroeber, *Gros Ventre Myths*, 71; Lowie, *The Assiniboine*, 111; and Skinner, *Notes on the Eastern Cree*, 86–87.

151 This story is compiled from de Jong, *Blackfoot Texts*, 6, 341; Little Chief, "History of the Blackfeet," 48–49; Uhlenbeck, *A New Series*, 192; and Wilson, *Wilson Papers*, 35–36.

152 James Willard Schultz, *Recently Discovered Tales of Life Among the Indians*, ed. Warren L. Hanna (Missoula: Mountain Press Publishing Company, 1988), 8; Kroeber, *Gros Ventre Myths*, 68–69; Chumak, *The Stonies*, 72; and Lowie, *The Assiniboine*, 116.

153 This story is compiled from Levern, "Notes"; Wissler and Duvall, *Mythology of the Blackfoot Indians*, 34; and Uhlenbeck, *A New Series*, 34.

154 De Jong, *Blackfoot Texts*, 23–28, and Kroeber, *Gros Ventre Myths*, 70–71.

155 This story is adapted from "Napi and the Beaver," by Kee-pi-poo-kiowa or Hundred Bear, in Blackfeet Community Education Program, *Blackfeet Cook Book*.

156 Lowie, *The Assiniboine*, 112; Chumak, *The Stonies*, 78.

157 This story is compiled from Wilson, *Wilson Papers*, 24–25; Grinnell, *Blackfeet Indian Stories*, 177; E.F. Wilson, "Report," 186; Uhlenbeck, *A New Series*, 167–68; and Mountain Horse, *My People*, 112–13.

158 Little Chief, "History of the Blackfeet," 56.

159 Lowie, *The Northern Shoshone*, 105.

160 This story is adapted from de Jong, *Blackfoot Texts*, 20–21.

161 Kroeber, *Gros Ventre Myths*, 76–77, and Robert H. Lowie, *Myths and Traditions of the Crow Indians* (New York: American Museum of Natural History, 1918), 49–50.

162 Grinnell, in *Blackfoot Lodge Tales*, 151, writes, "*Ni'-nah O-kai'-yu! Ni'-nah O-kai-yu! Nap'i I-nit'-si-wah! Nap'i I-nit'-si-wah!*"

163 This story is primarily adapted from Grinnell, *Blackfoot Lodge Tales*, 149–52; the ending line comes from James Willard Schultz, *Blackfeet Tales of Glacier National Park* (Boston: Houghton Mifflin Company, 1916), 127.

164 Schultz, *Blackfeet Tales*, 127, and Grinnell, *Blackfoot Lodge Tales*, 152.

165 Skinner, "Plains Cree Tales," 349.

166 This story is adapted from Ferris Smith, "(Na-be) The Old Man," Glenbow Archives, M2015.

# REFERENCES

Babcock-Abrahams, Barbara. "'A Tolerated Margin of Mess': The Trickster and his Tales Reconsidered." *Journal of the Folklore Institute* 11, no. 3 (1975): 147–86.

Ballinger, Franchot. "Living Sideways: Social Themes and Social Relationships in Native American Trickster Tales." *American Indian Quarterly* 13, no. 1 (Winter 1989): 15–30.

Blackfeet Community Education Program. *Blackfeet Cook Book*. Browning, MT: Blackfeet Community Education Program, 1969.

Black Plume, Cecil. "Adventures of Napi." *The Outlook* (Lethbridge), December 1972.

Bloomfield, Leonard. *Sacred Legends of the Sweet Grass Cree*. Bulletin No. 60. Ottawa: National Museum of Canada, 1930.

Boas, Franz. *Traditions of the Thompson River Indians of British Columbia*. New York: Houghton Mifflin, 1898.

Brinton, Daniel G. *Myths of the New World: A Treatise on the Symbolism and Mythology of the Red Race of America*. 1868. Philadelphia: David McKay, 1896.

Bullchild, Percy. *The Sun Came Down: The History of the World as My Blackfeet Elders Told It*. San Francisco: Harper and Row, 1985.

Carroll, Michael P. "Lévi-Strauss, Freud, and the Trickster: A New Perspective upon an Old Problem." *American Ethnologist* 8, no. 2 (May 1981): 301–13.

———. "The Trickster as Selfish-Buffoon and Culture Hero." *Ethos* 12, no. 2 (Summer 1984): 105–31.

Chumak, Sebastian. *The Stonies of Alberta: An Illustrated Heritage of Genesis, Myths, Legends, Folklore and Wisdom of Wichastabi, the People-Who-Cook-With-Hot-Stones*. Calgary: The Alberta Foundation, 1983.

———. *The Wisdom of the Blackfoot, the Bloods and the Peigans of Canada*. Toronto: Canada Heritage Foundation, 1988.

Coues, Elliott, Alexander Henry, and David Thompson. *New Light on the Early History of the Greater Northwest: The Manuscript Journals of Alexander Henry and of David Thompson, 1799–1814.* New York: Francis P. Harper, 1897.

de Jong, Jan Petrus Benjamin de Josselin. *Blackfoot Texts from the Southern Peigans Blackfoot Reservation, Teton County, Montana.* Amsterdam: Johannes Müller, 1914.

Dorsey, George A. *The Pawnee Mythology.* Carnegie Institution of Washington, pub. 59, 446, No. 126. Washington, DC, 1904.

Dorsey, George A,. and A.L. Kroeber. *Traditions of the Arapaho.* Vol. 101, no. 49. Chicago: Field Museum, Anthropological Publications, 1903.

Erdoes, Richard, and Alfonso Ortiz, eds. *American Indian Myths and Legends.* New York: Pantheon Books, 1984.

Ewers, John C. *The Horse in Blackfoot Indian Culture, with Comparative Material from Other Western Tribes.* Washington, DC: US Government Printing Office, 1955.

Fidler, Peter. *Journal of a Journey over Land from Buckingham House to the Rocky Mountains in 1792 & 3.* Hudson's Bay Company Archives, E.3/2, Provincial Archives of Manitoba.

Forbis, Richard G. *The Old Women's Buffalo Jump, Alberta.* Bulletin No. 180. Ottawa: National Museum of Canada, 1960.

Fraser, Frances. *The Wind Along the River.* Toronto: Macmillan, 1968.

———. *The Bear Who Stole the Chinook.* Toronto: Macmillan, 1959.

Freud, Sigmund. *Totem and Taboo: Resemblances between the Psychic Lives of Savages and Neurotics.* New York: Random House, 1918.

Frey, Rodney. *Stories that Make the World: Oral Literature of the Indian Peoples of the Inland Northwest.* Norman: University of Oklahoma Press, 1995.

Goddard, Pliny Earle. *Apache Texts.* Anthropological Papers of the American Museum of History, Vol. 8. New York: Published by Order of the Trustees, 1911.

Goldfrank, Esther S. "'Old Man' and the Father Image in Blood (Blackfoot) Society." In *Psychoanalysis and Culture,* ed. G.B. Wilbur and W. Muensterberger. New York: International Universities Press, 1951.

Grinnell, George Bird. *By Cheyenne Campfires.* Norman: University of Oklahoma Press, 1971.

———. *Blackfeet Indian Stories.* New York: Charles Scribner's Sons, 1913.

———. *Blackfoot Lodge Tales*. 1892. Lincoln: University of Nebraska Press, 1962.

———. *Blackfoot Lodge Tales: The Story of a Prairie People*. New York: Charles Scribner's Sons, 1892.

Hale, Horatio. "Report on the Blackfoot Tribes." *Report of the Committee . . . Appointed for the Purpose of Investigating and Publishing Reports on the Physical Characteristics, Languages, Industrial and Social Condition of the North-Western Tribes of the Dominion of Canada*. London: British Association of the Advancement of Science, September 1885.

Hoffman, Walter James. *The Menomini Indians*. Washington, DC: Bureau of American Ethnology, 1896.

Joe Little Chief Manuscripts. Joe Little Chief fonds, Glenbow Archives.

Jones, Karen R. *Wolf Mountains: A History of Wolves along the Great Divide*. Calgary: University of Calgary Press, 1995.

Jung, Carl G. *Four Archetypes: Mother, Rebirth, Spirit, Trickster*. Princeton: Princeton University Press, 1970.

Kenton, Edna, ed. *The Jesuit Relations and Allied Documents: Travels and Explorations of the Jesuit Missionaries in North America (1610–1791)*. New York: Vanguard Press, 1954.

Kroeber, A.L. *Gros Ventre Myths and Tales*. New York: American Museum of Natural History, 1907.

Lafitau, Joseph François. *Customs of the American Indians Compared with the Customs of Primitive Times*. Vol. 1. Ed. and trans. William N. Fenton and Elizabeth L. Moore. Toronto: The Champlain Society, 1974.

Levern, J.L. (1871–1960). "Notes et Souvenirs Concernant les Piednoirs." Manuscript. Microfilm No. 234, Glenbow Archives, Calgary.

Lévi-Strauss, Claude. "Structuralism and Ecology." In *Readings for a History of Anthropological Theory*, ed. Paul A. Erickson and Liam Donat Murphy. Toronto: University of Toronto Press, 2013. 161–74.

Linderman, Frank Bird. *Indian Why Stories*. New York: Charles Scribner's Sons, 1915.

———. *Indian Old-Man Stories*. New York: Charles Scribner's Sons, 1920.

———. *Old Man Coyote*. New York: John Day Company, 1931.

Little Bear, Ruth. "Indian Version of the Creation." *Kainai News* (southern Alberta), June 5, 1968.

Lopez, Barry Holstun. *Giving Birth to Thunder, Sleeping with his Daughter: Coyote Builds North America.* New York: Avon Books, 1977.

Lowie, Robert H. *The Assiniboine.* New York: American Museum of Natural History, 1909.

———. *Myths and Traditions of the Crow Indians.* New York: American Museum of Natural History, 1918.

———. "The Northern Cheyenne." Undated typescript, Glenbow Museum Archives.

———. *The Northern Shoshone.* New York: American Museum of Natural History, 1909.

McClintock, Walter. *Old Indian Trails.* Boston: Houghton Mifflin, 1923.

———. *The Old North Trail, Or, Life, Legends, and Religion of the Blackfeet Indians.* 1910. Lincoln, NB: University of Nebraska Press, 1999.

Maclean, John. "Blackfoot Mythology." *Journal of American Folk-Lore* 6, no. 22 (July-September 1893): 164–72.

Mountain Horse, Mike. *My People the Bloods.* Calgary: Glenbow-Alberta Institute and Blood Tribal Council, 1979.

Nelson, John. "Blackfoot Names of a Number of Places in the North-West Territory, for the Most Part in the Vicinity of the Rocky Mountains." *Report of Progress, 1882-83-84.* Appendix II. Ottawa: Geological and Natural History Survey and Museum of Canada, 1885.

Petitot, Émile. *Traditions indiennes du Canada nord-ouest.* Part 7: *Légendes et traditions des Pieds-Noirs au Canada,* 489–507. Paris: Maisonneuve frères et C. Leclerc, 1886.

Radin, Paul. *The Trickster: A Study in Native American Mythology.* New York: Schocken Books, 1972.

Ricketts, Mac Linscott. "The North American Indian Trickster." *History of Religions* 5, no. 2 (Winter, 1966): 327–50.

Rides at the Door, Darnell Davis. *Napi Stories.* Browning: Blackfeet Heritage Program, 1979.

Sanderville, Richard. "The Religion of the Blackfeet Indians." Anthropological Archives, file 4080. Smithsonian Institution, Washington, DC, 1934.

Schultz, James Willard. *Blackfeet Tales of Glacier National Park.* Boston: Houghton Mifflin Company, 1916.

———. *Recently Discovered Tales of Life Among the Indians.* Ed. Warren L. Hanna. Missoula: Mountain Press Publishing Co., 1988.

Siebelt, Dagmar. *Die Winter Counts der Blackfoot.* Munster: Lit Verlag, 2005.

Skinner, Alanson. *Notes on the Eastern Cree and Northern Saulteaux.* New York: American Museum of Natural History, 1911.

———. "Plains Cree Tales." *The Journal of American Folk-Lore* 29 (1916): 341–366.

Smith, Ferries. "(Na-be) The Old Man." Glenbow Archives, M2015.

Tailfeathers, Rick. "How the Mice Saved Christmas." *Kainai News* (southern Alberta), December 1-2, 1980, 28.

Taylor, Fraser. *Standing Alone: A Contemporary Blackfoot Indian.* Halfmoon Bay, BC: Arbutus Bay Publications, 1989.

Uhlenbeck, Christianus C. *Original Blackfoot Texts.* Amsterdam: Johannes Müller, 1911.

———. *A New Series of Blackfoot Texts.* Amsterdam: Johannes Müller, 1912.

White Bull, Jim. "The History of Great Temuelites or Blackfoot Nation. Their Indian God Old Man—Na-pee." n.d. Unpublished manuscript in author's possession.

Wilson, E.F. "Report on the Blackfoot Tribes." Report of the British Association for the Advancement of Science 57 (1887): 183–200.

Wilson, Robert N. *The R.N. Wilson Papers*, vol. 1, ed. Philip H. Godsell. Unpublished manuscripts. Part 1: "Notes and General Observations on the Blood Indians" (1–20). Part 2: "Myths and Legends" (22–112). Calgary: Glenbow Foundation, 1958.

Wissler, Clark, and David C. Duvall. *Mythology of the Blackfoot Indians.* Anthropological Papers of the American Museum of Natural History, vol. 2, part 1. New York: American Museum of Natural History, 1908.

# BOOKS BY HUGH A. DEMPSEY

*The Great Blackfoot Treaties* (Heritage House Publishing, 2015)

*Always an Adventure: An Autobiography* (University of Calgary Press, 2011)

*Maskepetoon: Leader, Warrior, Peacemaker* (Heritage House Publishing, 2010)

*The Vengeful Wife and Other Blackfoot Stories* (University of Oklahoma Press, 2003)

*Firewater: The Impact of the Whisky Trade on the Blackfoot Nation* (Fifth House Publishers, 2002)

*With Eagle Tail: Arnold Lupson and 30 Years Among the Sarcee, Blackfoot and Stoney Indians on the North American Plains*, co-authored with Colin F. Taylor (Smithmark/ Salamander Books Ltd., 1999)

*Indians of the Rocky Mountain Parks* (Fifth House Publishers, 1998)

*Tom Three Persons: Legend of an Indian Cowboy* (Purich Publishing, 1997)

*Tribal Honors: A History of the Kainai Chieftainship* (Kainai Chieftainship, 1997)

*The Golden Age of the Canadian Cowboy* (Fifth House Publishers, 1995)

*The Amazing Death of Calf Shirt and other Blackfoot Stories: Three Hundred Years of Blackfoot History* (Fifth House Publishers, 1994; University of Oklahoma Press, 1996)

*Calgary: Spirit of the West* (Fifth House Publishers, 1994)

*Treasures of the Glenbow Museum* (Glenbow Museum / Alberta Institute, 1991)

*Bibliography of the Blackfoot*, co-authored with Lindsay Moir (Scarecrow Press, 1989)

*The Gentle Persuader: A Biography of James Gladstone, Indian Senator* (Prairie Books, 1986)

*Big Bear: The End of Freedom* (Douglas & McIntyre / University of Nebraska Press, 1984)

*History in their Blood: The Indian Portraits of Nicholas de Grandmaison* (Douglas & McIntyre / Hudson Hills Press, 1982)

*Christmas in the West* (Prairie Books, 1982)

*Red Crow, Warrior Chief* (Prairie Books / University of Nebraska Press, 1980)

*Indian Tribes of Alberta* (Glenbow Museum, 1979)

*Charcoal's World: The True Story of a Canadian Indian's Last Stand* (Prairie Books / University of Nebraska Press, 1978)

*Crowfoot, Chief of the Blackfeet* (University of Oklahoma Press / Hurtig Publishers, 1972)

**Hugh A. Dempsey** is an author, historian, and researcher. He is the former associate director of the Glenbow Museum in Calgary, and is currently its chief curator emeritus. He is also the editor of the quarterly *Alberta History*. Dempsey was made an honorary chief of the Kainai Blackfoot in 1967 and in 1975 was invested as a member of the Order of Canada. He is the author of more than twenty books, including *The Great Blackfoot Treaties*, *Maskepetoon*, *Firewater*, and *Crowfoot*.

**Alyssa Koski**, a member of the Blood Tribe, is an illustrator who graduated from the Alberta College of Art and Design with a BA in Visual Communications. She is the recipient of the Janet Mitchell Award and the Harley Brown Artistic Endowment and the winner of the 2017 *Applied Arts Magazine* design award.